YOU'RE SO COLD I'M TURNIN' BLUE

MARTHA HUME'S GUIDE TO THE
GREATEST IN COUNTRY MUSIC

YOU'RE SO COLD I'M TURNIN' BLUE

MARTHA HUME

The Viking Press   *New York*

Penguin Books

Penguin Books Ltd, Harmondsworth, Middlesex, England
Penguin Books, 625 Madison Avenue, New York, New York 10022, U.S.A.
Penguin Books Australia Ltd, Ringwood, Victoria, Australia
Penguin Books Canada Limited, 2801 John Street, Markham, Ontario, Canada L3R 1B4
Penguin Books (N.Z.) Ltd, 182–190 Wairau Road, Auckland 10, New Zealand

First published in 1982 in simultaneous hardcover and paperback editions
by The Viking Press and Penguin Books, 625 Madison Avenue, New York, New York 10022
Published simultaneously in Canada

Library of Congress Cataloging in Publication Data
Hume, Martha.
  You're so cold I'm turnin' blue.
  1. Country music–United States–History and criticism.   I. Title.
ML3524.H85   1982   784.5′2′00973   82-70133
ISBN 0-670-24417-1 (hardbound)
ISBN 0 14 006.348 X (paperbound)

Grateful acknowledgment is made to the following for permission to reprint copyrighted material:
The Country Music Foundation: Photographs appearing on pages 7, 19, 20, 23 (right), 32 (left), 46 (left),
    61, 64, 110, 149 (above), 154–155, and 162 are used courtesy of the Country Music Foundation
    Library and Media Center, Nashville, Tennessee.
House of Cash: Selection from "Man in Black," by Johnny Cash. Copyright © 1971
    by Song of Cash, Inc. ASCAP. Used by permission.
Willie Nelson Music, Inc.: Selection from "It's Not Supposed to be That Way."
    Copyright © 1974 by Willie Nelson Music Company.
Peer International Corporation: Selection from "It Wasn't God Who Made Honky
    Tonk Angels," by J. D. Miller. Copyright 1952 by Peer International Corporation.
    Copyright renewed. Used by permission. All rights reserved.
Red River Dave McEnery: "The Ballad of Patty Hearst" copyright © 1974 by
    Red River Dave McEnery.
United Artists Music Co., Inc.: Selection from "You Never Even Called Me By My Name" by Steve
    Goodman. Copyright © 1971 by Kama Rippa Music, Inc. All rights administered by
    United Artists Music Co., Inc.

Cover/Jacket Art: Elvis wine bottle, TM and © Boxcar Enterprises, Inc. 1978. Distributed
    by Frontenac Vineyards.

Family trees on pages 35, 40, and 41 by Compass Projections.
Photo credits appear on page 203.

Printed in the United States of America
Set in Linotron Bookman
Designed by Ann Gold

God has blessed me with many friends—

this book is for all of you.

ACKNOWLEDGMENTS

The information contained in this book is the product of twelve years' worth of involvement with country music and country musicians. During that time, I've found that people who are involved in country music are among the most likable in the world. They've taken me into their homes, onto their touring buses, and into their hearts with a sometimes surprising alacrity. I've learned something from almost everybody, and finally, I have the chance to thank them publicly.

First, thanks to the Nitty Gritty Dirt Band and William McCuen who allowed me to observe country music history in the making during the recording sessions in 1971 for the album *Will The Circle Be Unbroken?* Those sessions mark the beginning of my understanding of and interest in country music. Second, thanks to Kinky Friedman, Hazel Smith, Waylon Jennings, Jessi Colter, Tompall Glaser, and everyone at "Hillbilly Central" who taught me about the guts of country music and about the goodness of its people. Third, thanks to Loretta Lynn, who taught me about myself.

And thanks to Chet Flippo, my husband, who put up with me while I was learning all of this. I love you all.

My agent, Peter Matson, my editors, William Strachan and Vicki Stein, and my friends at The Viking Press and Penguin Books have seen to it that what was too often a hopelessly jumbled mess of information became a book. My friend Stephanie Chernikowski was always available as a sounding board for ideas and her criticism was always valuable. My gratitude to all of you.

Many other people contributed in one way and another to *You're So Cold I'm Turnin' Blue,* and I wish to include you all as well:

In Nashville: Robert Oermann, Ron Pugh, Bob Pinson and the staff of the Country Music Foundation; Bobby and Jeannie Bare; Doug Green, Dolly Parton, Billy Joe Shaver, Elizabeth Thiels, Laura Eipper Hill, Lorene Allen, Sheriff Fate Thomas, Bill Monroe, Tammy Wynette, George Jones, Chet Atkins, Rosanne Cash, Rodney Crowell, Captain Midnite, Alene Jackson, L. E. White, Conway Twitty, Jim Webb,

Cindy Rose, Ernest Tubb, Earl Scruggs, Don Warden, Jerry Bradley, Owen Bradley, Helen Farmer, Jo Anne Walker and the staff of the Country Music Association, and Mrs. Edna Bloodworth and the staff of the Spence Manor Hotel.

In Kentucky: Mrs. C. W. Hume, Hannah Baird, Dr. Bill Burge, Charlie, Noah and Hazel Kinney; Loyal Jones, Lilly May Ledford, Pearl and Shelby Martin, Carolyn and Wally Bates, Mrs. Ruth Turner, Wade and Julia Mainer, and James Roberts.

In New York: Mort Cooperman, Bill Dick, Don Reynolds and the staff of The Lone Star Cafe, Paula Batson, Charlyn Zlotnick,
Speed Vogel, Lois Anselowitz, Lauren Agnelli, Nick Tosches, Greg Geller, Sim Meyers, Susan Toepfer, Katie Valk, and Augie Meyer.

In California: Grelun Landon, David and Sandy Brokaw, Kris Kristofferson, Bob Larson, Michael Apted, Billy Swan, and Michael Ochs.

In Texas: Doug and Jan Hanners, Huey Meaux, Doug Sahm, Willie and Connie Nelson, Floyd Tillman, and Barbara Thornton.

Elsewhere: Bill Carter, Benton Carter, Les Paul, Aline Guillot, Levon and Sandy Helm, Leon McAuliffe, and Smokey Dacus.

Thanks to all of you.

PREFACE

Most writing about country music falls into one of three categories. There are scholarly histories and biographies, like Bill Malone's *Country Music, U.S.A.* and Nolan Porterfield's *Jimmie Rodgers*; popular "star" autobiographies, such as Loretta Lynn's *Coal Miner's Daughter* and Tammy Wynette's *Stand By Your Man*; and there are quasi-journalistic, quasi-sociological books—often anthologies—like Peter Guralnick's *Lost Highway: Journeys and Arrivals of American Musicians* and Paul Hemphill's *Bright Lights and Country Music: The Nashville Sound*. In addition to these genres there are also many collections of song folios, of use mainly to the person who wants to learn some of the music for his own enjoyment, and there is the stray piece of fiction, almost always poorly executed.

While I have found much to enjoy in books from each of these categories, I haven't found any one that reflects my personal understanding of country music and its world. The histories, certainly valuable pieces of scholarship, are joyless and te-dious. The star autobiographies are often fun to read and are of value as social documents, but since they pertain to individual experiences, they cannot be used to learn about the music in general. The anthologies are better, but too often the separate pieces lack a context. With this book, I am trying to provide that context in a way that is neither too scholarly nor too tedious, and in a way that I hope will be fun to read.

It is possible to understand some forms of popular music without knowing anything of the singer or of the song's composer, or of the song's background. But country music songs sound the way they do and convey the messages they do because they come not only from individual songwriters but from a culture that is unique to country music. Not since the days of movie studio contract players has there been a community of performers so closely connected by geography, by common institutions and values, by a common outlook on life, and by a common history. Knowing something of this community and its customs adds immeasurably to one's understanding of the music produced by that community.

It's commonly noted, for example, that country songs are often sad; but why? Why is Johnny Cash constantly singing about trains and jails? Why is the Grand Ole Opry such a big deal? What kind of a world produces Dolly Parton? How can one tell if a specific song is "country" or some other kind of music? These are the kinds of questions that most other writers address only indirectly, if at all. Perhaps it's because other writers live closer to the center of the culture than I do, but the fact that country music *is* a culture, in every sense of that word, is usually overlooked.

I didn't begin to see country music in this way myself until I had spent nearly ten years as a music journalist; then, gradually, I began to see the differences between country musicians and other musicians. Rock and roll bands, for example, are self-contained units while the band is traveling. When not on tour, however, the individual members scatter to the four winds. Country bands are also self-contained while traveling, but when the tour is over, the great majority of the musicians go home to Nashville, Tennessee. Rock musicians may know only a few other musicians outside their own bands; country musicians all know each other—and usually know an amazing amount about each other's business. There is a social and political hierarchy among country musicians that isn't present among other musicians. One learns that there are certain things one can talk to a country star about and certain things one can't. There are usually certain unspoken standards of behavior one should observe in the country music community, certain ways business is done. While other pop musicians won't set foot on a stage without all sorts of complicated contracts being signed, a country star will often appear on the ba-

sis of a handshake with the promoter. Most rock and roll stars wouldn't dream of giving an autograph to the average fan. I have seen country stars—even the most successful ones—stay as long as two hours after a performance so that everyone who wants to has a chance to get an autograph and a word with the performer. All of this is because, over the years, country musicians have established a certain way of doing things, a certain way of looking at life, and a certain way of living with other people that is unique to country music. An explanation of how this came to be is in order.

When commercial country music began in the twenties, there were individual performers in locations ranging from New York to Chicago to Atlanta to eastern Virginia, to Kentucky to Tennessee to Texas. What we now think of as country music was then no more than a few songs sung by a few self-trained musicians on a few records. The music itself matured with its contemporary, radio, which, beginning about 1923, began to present country music programs, usually called "barn dances," to an audience that was largely white and largely rural. At that time, country music was not so much Southern music as it was rural music. There were many radio barn dance programs, beginning, apparently, with either a program on WSB in Atlanta or a barn dance show on WBAP in Fort Worth in 1923. The barn dance format was soon adopted by WLS, Sears Roebuck's station in Chicago. Originally called "The Chicago Barn Dance," this show became the influential "National Barn Dance." In 1925, station WSM in Nashville started its "WSM Barn Dance" using the same format as the Chicago program. This show evolved into the famous "Grand Ole Opry," but at that time the Opry was only one of many such shows. There were equally popular radio broadcasts on WSB in Atlanta; WCKY in Covington, Kentucky; WLW in Cincinnati, Ohio; WWVA in Wheeling, West Virginia; and on powerful XERA, the Mexican border station outside Del Rio, Texas. For a time, almost every radio station of any size had a country music program, and there were country-style musicians all over America.

Very, very gradually, however, WSM's Grand Ole Opry began to gain an edge over the other barn dance shows. Under the direction of George D. Hay, who, as "the Solemn Old Judge," was also the program's announcer, the Opry picked up outstanding talent from the beginning. Originally a 1,000-watt station, WSM became a "clear-channel" 50,000-watt station in 1939. The same year, the part of the show sponsored by Prince Albert Tobacco was picked up by NBC's "Red Network," and by 1940, the Opry could be heard in most parts of the country. With talent that included, by 1941, Uncle Dave Macon, Pee Wee King and the Golden West Cowboys, Bill Monroe, Roy Acuff, Minnie Pearl, and Ernest Tubb, the Opry soon became unstoppable.

By 1950 the Opry was supreme among country music radio shows, and Nashville had become the place where an aspiring country music star had to go if he or she was to be successful. In recognition of the Opry's success and its talent pool, major record companies established recording studios and offices in Nashville, beginning with Decca in 1945. RCA and Columbia soon followed. The records gave Opry stars more exposure and stars of other barn dance shows found that if they wanted recording contracts, Nashville was the only place to go. The town rapidly became the geographic center of country music. The Ryman Auditorium, where the Opry moved in 1941, became known as "the Mother Church of Country Music." Nashville, which once proudly claimed to be "the Athens of the South" (and which has a full-size repro-

duction of the Parthenon to prove it), came to be known as "Music City, U.S.A." Aside from a few western swing bands in California, a country music act soon found that it could not survive in any style without some contact with Nashville and, if possible, the Opry. The only wonder of the whole affair is that the Opry's management never saw fit to start a record label of its own. Had it done so, the Grand Ole Opry would have had an absolute monopoly on the production of country music for years to come.

As it was, the Opry was powerful enough during the 1950s. The management looked on its stars not as independent contractors but as employees. Performers, when they were finally paid, received only union scale, and they were expected to be onstage at the Opry for a specified number of Saturday nights every year. The Opry management felt that the exposure gained by being on the show more than made up for the low pay, because performers could then get so many personal appearance bookings just by virtue of being members of the Opry. Moreover, Opry members were expected to represent the Opry at all times by being clean, neat, sober, God-fearing, chaste, and patriotic. These standards created problems for Opry stars. On the one hand, they had to endure grueling road tours to make money—tours that were often so difficult that many performers found liquor and pills a necessity if they were to continue. On the other hand, they had to be back in Nashville every Saturday night to be on the Opry. If they didn't show up, or showed up drunk or stoned, they would be dismissed, and dismissal from the Opry meant an effective end to one's career as a country star of any magnitude. Thus, the country singer usually had to hide his real personality from everyone except his closest friends and family. Since country singers were treated very much like children, it is no wonder that many of them tended to be irresponsible in their personal lives. Perhaps Hank Williams, who died in the back of his powder-blue Cadillac on New Year's Eve, 1953, the victim of booze and pills, was made to die, not born to die.

Second in command of the country star's career was the singer's record label. Although record company executives usually did not act *in loco parentis,* as did the Opry management, staff producers determined an artist's style and sound. No matter what a performer sounded like live, he or she would sound like a staff producer's creature on record. The last person to offer ideas about what kind of a record to make was often the singer himself. This situation would spawn the "outlaw" movement of the early 1970s, but in the 1950s, no one seemed to protest.

And so there came to be a large group of musicians and singers, all of whom lived in the same place, all of whom sang the same kind of music, many of whom worked for the same employer and played the same places out of town, and most of whom came from the same backgrounds. Country singers tended to come from the South or Southwest, and most were white (although Deford Bailey, one of the Opry's first members, was black). Many came from families who'd lived in impoverished circumstances; most were of the Protestant faith, and many of these were fundamentalists. It is little wonder that a common culture was born, for these people, so alike, were isolated, even in Nashville, where the non-music-business citizenry tended to look down on the "hillbilly" musicians from whom Nashville derived so much of its municipal revenue.

This culture had its myths—the wandering Jimmie Rodgers; the tormented Hank Williams; the virtuous singing cowboy in his white hat. It had a history, beginning in the 1920s and continuing through the present. It had a power structure made up of the Opry management, the record companies, the music-industry business community, the more established stars, and then on down through the ranks of lower-level singers, pickers, and songwriters, through the auxiliary people who serviced the business. It had a code of behavior based on Southern fundamentalism and the Opry's standards. And it had as its purpose to act as the spokesman for the "common man." Its philosophy was that of the American rural populace: all men are equal, no one higher than anyone else. Its motto might have been, "Don't get above your raisin'," which means that you should never put on airs, no matter how high in life you may rise. To some extent, this culture endures today, if through nothing else than the music itself, where one can find the culture's beliefs and aspirations written in the words of the songs.

Nonetheless, country music seems likely to fall victim to the American tide of homogenization. Rural people are now little different from suburban people; Southerners watch the same television shows as Northerners. Nashville is no longer an isolated outpost for a specific kind of performer, but a modern recording center for musicians of all persuasions. The Opry's power is seriously waning, which is good, in a way, but bad in the sense that it is becoming little more than a museum for music that is no longer relevant to the American experience. To turn the music of America's hopes and dreams and pains into an amusement park—which is where the Opry is now housed—is very sad, even if the new Opry house does have dressing rooms.

None of this necessarily means that there will be no more country music. Its specialty no longer has much to do with the "country" part of the name anyway. Instead, country music addresses itself to the everyday concerns of its audience, and the music will change only as the concerns of that audience change. When most listeners were farmers, country singers sang about farming. When the audience moved to the city and worked in factories, there were songs about the assembly line. It is more than probable that there will be a country song about a computer pretty soon. And even if circumstances change, life doesn't. Success, failure, love, despair, hope, and the problem of living from one day to the next will always be with us. These things are country music's specialties. Fantasies are left to other kinds of singers, other kinds of music. In this sense there will always be a country music community.

Reading this book won't tell you everything you need to know about country music. No book can ever convey information about any kind of music the way that the music itself can, and one should begin the study of country music there, with the music. Having done that, this book may help you to understand and appreciate that music better. Some of the material you will read is quite straightforward. Some of it is definitely tongue-in-cheek. Some of it was given to me in complete trust by country musicians of all kinds, many of whom welcomed me into their homes and into their confidence. For that reason, specific names are not always mentioned, for I can't violate confidences so freely given.

I hope that I have managed to convey how much I really love country music and how much enjoyment I've gotten from the music and its people. If that comes through, and if some of you come to feel that same love and that same sense of fun, then this book will have succeeded.

Martha Hume
New York, New York
January, 1982

CONTENTS

YOU'RE SO COLD I'M TURNIN' BLUE

WE CALL IT "COUNTRY"

What is now called "country music" has, at various times, been called "hillbilly music," "folk music," "country and western music," and just plain "Southern music." Moreover, as many as a dozen discrete styles of American music—ranging from Cajun to rockabilly to western swing—have been classified as country music at one time or another. It's no wonder that one of the longest-running arguments in the country music community has concerned the problem of what is or isn't country music.

If you need convincing that this is so, get some friends together and play the following ten songs, as recorded by the performers listed. Then try to figure out what makes each song "country." Is it the singer? The song? The band? The region where the song was recorded? The "message"?

"Blue Yodel Number One (T for Texas)" by Jimmie Rodgers
"Wreck on the Highway" sung by Roy Acuff
"Blue Moon of Kentucky" sung by Bill Monroe
"New San Antonio Rose" played by Bob Wills and his Texas Playboys
"Blue Moon of Kentucky" sung by Elvis Presley
"Jole Blon" sung by the Boisec Brothers
"He'll Have to Go" sung by Jim Reeves
"The Race Is On" sung by George Jones
"Honky Tonk Women" sung by Waylon Jennings
"Jessica" performed by the Allman Brothers Band

All these songs are "country" songs—even "Honky Tonk Women," which was written by Rolling Stones Mick Jagger and Keith Richards. The styles of country music that they represent are (in order): country blues, country gospel, bluegrass, western swing, rockabilly, Cajun, the Nashville Sound, honky tonk, outlaw country, and Southern rock. What ties them together? What makes them country?

If your answer to that question is "nothing," you're almost right, but not quite. The usual definition of country music is a song form distinguished either by the kinds of instruments used to play it or by the supposed "simplicity" of its lyrics. The latter

Texts, 1912. Country music's original audience was largely white and rural.

Right: *New York City, 1980. Today's country audience is often urban, educated, and sophisticated.*

explanation is hogwash. Compared to some rhythm and blues songs, for example, many country lyrics are far from simple. The instrumentation definition does have some validity—all the songs I listed are played by bands that use stringed instruments almost exclusively. Drums, where present, play with the bass; brass sections are nearly unheard of. Conversely, the steel guitar, which is used in many of these arrangements, is almost never heard in a pop song.

I think the problem of definition is better approached by looking at the country music audience. Throughout its history, country music, with all its styles and subgenres, has usually appealed to a cohesive group of people with certain attitudes and lifestyles in common. Unlike rock and roll, which often works as a force to change the way its audience thinks or feels, country music serves to validate ideas and attitudes already extant. Country music has been a unifying force, an expression of "we are all alike."

The music changed only as the audience changed. A song about divorce, for example, would have seemed blasphemous to the Carter Family audience, but to people who migrated to the industrial centers of the North during World War II, a song about divorce was merely a song about what was happening to them and their friends all the time. Similarly, a song by the Allman Brothers might sound like so much noise to people who grew up in the early fifties, but to their children, the same song would sound like a perfect melding of the country music favored by their parents and the rock music they heard on the radio. To this audience, the Carter Family sounds quaint. Thus, the question of which music qualifies as "country" is relative to what the country audience will accept.

What, then, is the country audience? Until very recently, the country music audience was made up of people who were born and raised in rural settings in the South or Southwest or people whose families had migrated to Northern cities from rural areas in the South. In general, this audience was made up of working-class white people, who were patriotic, politically and religiously conservative, and who believed—or professed to believe—in the "old-fashioned" virtues. When these people heard Merle Haggard's hippie-baiting "Okie From Muskogee," they took the song seriously.

Recently, this audience has broadened to include people from large cities, from all regions of America and several foreign countries, and from all social classes. In New York City, for example, one of the most popular radio stations among the residents of Chinatown is WHN, the country station. Predictably, country music itself has altered its style to accommodate the wider audience, and many modern country singers are difficult to distinguish from singers of "soft rock."

All of this makes for a rather puzzling definition of country music. To wit: country music is the music listened to by people who like country music.

On the other hand, it is possible to define specific styles that country music has drawn upon and that still can be heard in the music of many country singers, thus arriving at a definition of the music as the sum of its parts. The following glossary of various styles that have been classified as "country" will give you a pretty fair idea of the disparate elements that combine to form what we call country music.

THE BAKERSFIELD SOUND

Simply put, the Bakersfield Sound is the music played by a group of musicians who lived in and around Bakersfield, California, in the late fifties and early sixties, including Buck Owens, Merle Haggard, and Wynn

Merle Haggard, born with the Bakersfield sound.

Stewart. In contrast to its contemporary country cousin, the Nashville Sound, music made in Bakersfield was rawer, incorporating the steel guitar of pickers like Ralph Mooney, and also more rhythmic, including many elements of rockabilly music. The success of musicians such as Owens and Haggard marked the first time that country music produced in California became popular on a national level, and that success, in turn, marked the beginning of the end of Nashville's complete hegemony over the production of country music, a trend that also influenced the development of the outlaw movement of the seventies.

BLUEGRASS

Many people think that bluegrass is a very old form of country music, but while its roots do go back to the sound of mountain string bands, bluegrass itself is a relatively modern style. The name is taken from the name of Bill Monroe's band, the Bluegrass Boys (so named because Monroe comes from Kentucky, "the Bluegrass State"), and Monroe is usually credited with being the inventor, or the father of bluegrass music. The chief difference between bluegrass and the string band music that preceded it is the emphasis that bluegrass musicians place on rhythm and on instrumental virtuosity. For this reason bluegrass is often compared to jazz, but the style has remained strictly country because even modern bluegrass bands still use stringed instruments exclusively, and because the lyrical content of bluegrass is very similar to that of classic country music.

Bill Monroe, "the Father of Bluegrass Music."

The bluegrass singing style, often called "the high lonesome sound" and best exemplified by the Stanley Brothers' work, was a major influence on rockabilly musicians like Elvis Presley and Jerry Lee Lewis. Later, after Lester Flatt and Earl Scruggs repopularized bluegrass by playing on college campuses, a new generation of musicians, ranging from the Grateful Dead to Gram Parsons to Emmylou Harris, again incorporated bluegrass influences into popular music.

CAJUN

The word "Cajun" is a corruption of "Acadia," the name of an area in eastern Canada that includes Nova Scotia and New Brunswick, where French colonials settled in the early eighteenth century. The French, exiled from the region after the French and Indian War, traveled south to settle in southern Louisiana, which was then a French colony under Napoleon. The descendants of these settlers who still live in the area are called Cajuns, as is the music made by native musicians.

Cajun music incorporates many elements of the French culture of the region, not the least of which is that it is usually sung in the local patois, which is a corrupt form of the French language. In addition, many Cajun bands include both an accordion player and a fiddler, and most songs are played in a simple three-quarter waltz time. No performer who plays music that is strictly Cajun has ever been a success in commercial country music, but Cajun-influenced musicians such as Moon Mullican, Jimmy C. Newman, and Doug and Rusty Kershaw have had country hits with Cajun-influenced songs. "Jole Blon" is the best-known Cajun country song, and it has been recorded by many non-Cajun musicians.

CONJUNTO

Conjunto, which simply means "band" in Spanish, is another very distant relative of country music. Stylistically, the term is used in Mexico and southern Texas to refer to a style of music popular along the border between Mexico and the United States. Conjunto musicians have incorporated elements of both Cajun and German music, the latter from music played by area roadbuilders, who were mostly German. There is usually an accordion player in conjunto bands, while the music is played in either waltz or polka time. Although the music remains a regional form, musicians like Doug Sahm and Augie Meyer were heavily influenced by the sound, as was Freddy Fender (Baldemar Huerta), whose recording of "Wasted Days and Wasted Nights" is an example of what might be called country conjunto.

COUNTRY BLUES

"Country blues" is often used as a code phrase to refer to the music made by white singers who have incorporated black music into their style. Jimmie Rodgers is the most famous of these singers, but many country musicians—Hank Williams, Bill Monroe, all of the rockabilly performers, Ronnie Milsap, and even Willie Nelson—have adopted elements of black music into more traditional country styles. Country music's debt to black music is great, and is not recognized enough. Only gospel music rivals it in influence.

COUNTRY ROCK

Another hybrid, "country rock" can mean anything from country songs sung with rock and roll instrumentation to rock songs sung by country singers, to country songs sung by rock singers, to country music sung by anyone who isn't from the country. Classic country rock is generally acknowledged to have been created by Gram Parsons, who, with the International Submarine Band, the Byrds, the Flying Burrito Brothers, and, later, Emmylou Harris, united elements of both styles, but especially country vocal styles with rock rhythms, to create what he reportedly hoped would be something more than a synthesis of the two.

Strictly speaking, many of Parsons' songs

The late Gram Parsons helped make country music popular with young audiences in the late sixties, and started a trend called "country rock."

Jimmie Rodgers, who fused rural black blues with rural white musical styles, is known as "the Father of Country Music."

were more country than anything coming out of Nashville at the time, but his reputation as a rock performer helped bring country music to the attention of many rock bands, and did much to spur the California singer/songwriter trend that produced Jackson Browne, Linda Ronstadt and the Eagles. In the South, the effect was the opposite, in that it encouraged musicians who might have been expected to produce country music to fuse it with rock elements, leading to the "Southern rock" sound of the Allman Brothers, the Marshall Tucker Band, and the Charlie Daniels Band. Parsons' country rock also helped spur the Texas music style of the seventies.

COUNTRY AND WESTERN

Ernest Tubb is said to have conducted a one-man campaign in the late forties to have the term "hillbilly music" outlawed in favor of what he called "country-western music," on the basis that the latter term was more dignified. This term was legitimized in 1949, when *Billboard,* the music industry's leading trade magazine, changed the name of its "folk music" charts to "country and western." Although there was never much "western" about country and western, the term was used to apply to all forms of country music until the early seventies. Now "country and western" has been supplanted by the term "country."

FOLK MUSIC

The term "folk music" should be divided into urban folk and country folk. The latter refers to songs that have been passed down orally from generation to generation, usually originating with songs sung in Europe, especially Britain and Germany. Country folk songs are usually based on stories and are often sung without instrumental accompaniment. Bradley Kincaid, "the Kentucky Mountain Boy," was one of the first

country performers to collect these songs and use them commercially. The Carter Family also included many folk tunes in its repertoire, but A. P. Carter took credit for writing many of them, while Kincaid did not.

Urban folk music includes many of the older country folk tunes, and its musicians use country stringed instruments and arrangements. More often than not, however, urban "folkies" use the music to make political points. Exponents of this form include Woody Guthrie, Pete Seeger, Joan Baez, and Bob Dylan. The revival of interest in folk

music in the sixties did lead to the rediscovery of many traditional folk performers, like Doc Watson, Lilly May Ledford, Jean Ritchie, and even Bradley Kincaid. Eventually, this interest created a new respect for older performers and their music, as evidenced in projects like the Nitty Gritty Dirt Band's *Will the Circle Be Unbroken?* album made in 1971.

Ernest Tubb on his touring bus. Tubb crusaded to make country music respectable.

GOSPEL MUSIC

Like blues, gospel music can be divided into white gospel and black gospel. Gospel music is religious music, sung in an emotional, exhortative style, using whatever instruments are at hand. While black gospel is the more energetic and rhythmic of the two, white gospel has had more influence on country music; its singing style is much more forceful than the traditional monotonous, droning country style. Thus, gospel-influenced singers like Roy Acuff, Wilma Lee and Stoney Cooper, and Bill Monroe changed country vocal styles completely with their music, and incidentally helped to make the solo country singer a truly important figure in commercial music, an event that led to the creation of a star system.

HARD COUNTRY

Hard country music is the closest modern equivalent to old-fashioned gospel music. This term is applied to the work of singers like George Jones and is most prevalent among honky tonk musicians. In general, hard country makes no concessions to fad or fashion, uses classic country instruments (usually amplified), and features the singer rather than the music or the song. It is occasionally used as a synonym for "classic country," meaning music that has not been adulterated by rock or blues styles.

HILLBILLY MUSIC

No longer in fashion, the term "hillbilly" was once used to refer to all country music. The origin of the term is obscure, although it was first used in print in 1900, spelled as "hillbillie." Eventually, hillbilly came to be considered a derogatory word, and many country musicians resented being called hillbillies. Ernest Tubb was the most vocal of the word's opponents, and his efforts to change the music's name to "country and

George Jones is hailed as "the World's Greatest Country Singer." His face—and his voice—define the term "hard country."

western" were successful. The various civil rights movements of the sixties, which led to linguistic reforms as well as legal ones, inspired one wag to create a new song, titled: "Don't Call Us Hillbillies; We're Mountain Williams Now."

HONKY TONK MUSIC

Like hillbilly, the origin of the phrase "honky tonk" is unknown, though it is certainly Southern and probably black. The term was first used in a song title in 1937, but it didn't become widespread until the 1940s. Originally, honky tonk referred to a sleazy bar—a joint—and it is still used occasionally today to refer to any bar where country music is played.

Applied to a style of music, honky tonk originally meant any music played in a honky tonk. Since these bars were usually noisy and crowded, musicians began to use amplified instruments when playing the joints, so the music could be heard over the noise of the crowd. Moreover, since bar patrons were not overly interested in hearing songs about Mama and home, bands that played honky tonks began to write songs about the patrons' real concerns—adultery, divorce, rootlessness, and getting drunk. Ernest Tubb was one of the most famous of the early honky tonk musicians, and he was followed by performers such as Lefty Frizzell, Hank Williams, George Jones, Buck Owens, Merle Haggard, Hank Thompson, and Gary Stewart. Today honky tonk music is often confused with hard country, although it is actually a subgenre of that form.

THE NASHVILLE SOUND

Like its contemporary the Bakersfield Sound, the Nashville Sound is technically the style played by a certain group of musicians who worked in Nashville in the late fifties and early sixties. Because record companies did not allow individual performers to use their own bands and producers while making a record, and because Chet Atkins, who headed RCA Records, had such a large roster of talent to produce, the same group of session musicians were used to play on record after record that came out of Nashville at the time. Consequently, instrumental arrangements became both predictable and standardized, and the records began to have a common sound.

The Nashville Sound, when compared to the country music that had preceded it, was slick and sophisticated—leading to the adoption of yet another term to describe it—"countrypolitan." Examples of the sound can be found in the work of Nashville musicians such as Webb Pierce, Floyd Cramer, and the pre-"El Paso" Marty Robbins, but it is best exemplified in the work of the late Jim Reeves.

OLD TIME MUSIC

This term—sometimes rendered as "old timey"—refers to precommercial country music, both instrumental and vocal, and to the work of modern musicians who play in the old styles. It is sometimes used interchangeably with the term country folk music.

OUTLAW COUNTRY

Technically, there is no such thing as outlaw country music, even though appearances by Waylon Jennings or Willie Nelson are sometimes described in advertisements as "the Outlaw Sound." Moreover, the term should be dropped now, because there is no longer an outlaw movement in country music.

Originally, the word "outlaw" was applied to country music (probably by songwriter Hazel Smith, who worked for Tompall Glaser during the early seventies) to describe a loose-

Two of country's "outlaws"— David Allan Coe and Waylon Jennings.

knit group of musicians, including Jennings, Nelson, Glaser, Billy Joe Shaver, Kris Kristofferson, and others, who objected to the common Nashville practice of awarding creative control of recording sessions to the record company's staff producers rather than to the artists themselves. When this situation prevailed, a powerful staff producer—a Chet Atkins or a Billy Sherrill, for example—not only picked the songs the musician would perform on record, but picked the sidemen and wrote the arrangements as well. Therefore, a musician's record might have nothing at all to do with the way he or she sounded live, and the musician's ideas about how he *ought* to sound were often dismissed.

Jennings, Glaser, and company decided to work outside this system—hence the term "outlaw"—by pressuring the record companies to give artists control over their own work. Having done this, the outlaws surprised nearly everyone in the Nashville music business establishment by producing some of the best work of their careers. These records sold equally well to the non-country market and the traditional country core audience. Ironically, the outlaw moniker did not become widely known until Jerry Bradley, RCA's vice-president in charge of Nashville operations, came up with the idea of packaging some old tracks made by Jennings, Nelson, Glaser, and Jessi Colter under the title *The Outlaws*. It proved to be a stroke of marketing genius, and *The Outlaws* became the first country album to be certified platinum by the Recording Industry Association of America.

Today, most of the people who fought the record companies ten years ago are solidly established in the business and have no need to rebel about anything. So, *sic transit outlaw*.

PROGRESSIVE COUNTRY

This term, like "outlaw," has more to do with a movement than with music. "Progressive country" usually is used to describe any kind of country music played by the outlaws. The term apparently was coined in Texas during the early seventies, when young, long-haired musicians first began to mix with straight country musicians at places like the Armadillo World Headquarters in Austin. Progressive country music is often not progressive at all, but traditional. Asleep at the Wheel, for example, is considered a progressive country band because its members are young and some of the male musicians have long hair. On the other hand, Asleep at the Wheel did more to revive interest in classic western swing music of the late thirties and early forties than any dozen traditional country bands could have done. A term that is sometimes used interchangeably with progressive country is "redneck rock," which again refers to the seventies phenomenon of hippies mixing with rednecks, both musically and socially. Like "outlaw," both the terms "progressive country" and "redneck rock" have outlived their usefulness and should be retired.

ROCKABILLY

Despite the fact that, in his later years, Elvis Presley had about as much to do with rockabilly as Leonard Bernstein, his death gave impetus to a revival of interest in rockabilly music among young white teenagers, both here and in England.

Strictly speaking, rockabilly was a musical phenomenon of the decade between 1950 and 1960. In its simplest sense, the phrase refers to a combination of rock—or rhythm and blues—and hillbilly music—or country—which formed a hybrid that was more than the synthesis of the two. The best-known rockabilly musicians came from Sam Phillips' Sun Record Company in Memphis, and included Presley, Jerry Lee Lewis, Carl Perkins, Johnny Cash, Charlie

Rockabilly's "Million Dollar Quartet"—Jerry Lee Lewis, Carl Perkins, Johnny Cash, and Elvis Presley—at Sun Studios, in Memphis.

Rich, and Jack Clement. Other rockabilly acts—some of them very fine ones—did exist, and included the brilliant Rock and Roll Trio with Johnny and Dorsey Burnette, Little Jimmy Dickens, the Everly Brothers, Sleepy LaBeef, Eddie Cochran, the Collins Kids, and many others. Buddy Holly's earliest recorded work also qualifies as rockabilly music, but Holly seemed to be heading toward a very different sound at the time of his death, and had he lived, might not have been included in this group.

SINGING COWBOY MUSIC

This term hasn't very much to do with mainstream country music, but it is lumped in with country anyway. It refers to the music of the singing cowboys like Gene Autry and the Sons of the Pioneers, which was usually written specifically for movies in the thirties and forties. Because many country stars eventually began to dress like movie cowboys, even while not sounding like movie cowboys at all, the "western" part of country and western was added in the late 1940s. Often, the songs sung by cowboys in the movies were arranged for an orchestra, and it's probable that these were the first country songs to be accompanied by strings (i.e., violins and violas), a practice that many hard country fans still view with disdain.

SOUTHERN ROCK

This is another rather nebulous but widely used country music phrase, which was probably coined to describe the work of the Allman Brothers Band before Duane Allman's

Roy Rogers. He and Gene Autry are America's most famous singing cowboys. Inset: The Texas sound was born at Austin's Armadillo World Headquarters. Here, Texas football coach Darrell Royal, artist Jim Franklin, Billy Joe Shaver, and Waylon Jennings exhibit some Texas solidarity backstage.

death. Later it was used to categorize bands like Black Oak Arkansas, Lynyrd Skynyrd, the Marshall Tucker Band, and what seemed like dozens of semi-rock, semi-country, semi-jazz bands from south of the Mason-Dixon line. Gram Parsons and the Flying Burrito Brothers, the pioneers of country rock, are credited with being the role models for the musicians who would eventually play Southern rock. Currently, Alabama, a very popular country quartet, is carrying the very tattered and bedraggled banner of Southern rock.

STRING BAND MUSIC

Very simply, this refers to bands that use stringed instruments, as opposed to horns or drums, to make music. Most of the original country bands were string bands, favoring the guitar, the banjo, the mandolin, and the fiddle. On the other hand, many rockabilly bands could be called string bands because they often consisted of nothing more than two guitars and a standup bass, which provided the rhythm. For many years the Grand Ole Opry allowed only string bands on its stage, and even today, a simple snare drum is usually the only rhythm instrument used.

THE TEXAS SOUND

This term is practically synonymous with progressive country and redneck rock. It refers to any band from Texas, and thus has very little to do with the sound itself, since Texas bands play everything from polka music to acid rock.

TEX-MEX COUNTRY

Nationally, only one country star could be said to be making Tex-Mex country music, and that's Freddy Fender. On a local level, there is a Tex-Mex sound to be heard in towns like Austin and San Antonio, where some young musicians have organized bands using accordions and bajo sextos (six-stringed basses) to produce a hybrid conjunto sound. Elements of the Tex-Mex influence are found in rock music in the recorded work of the Sir Douglas Quintet, the father of Tex-Mex rock and roll.

WESTERN SWING

The original members of the best western swing bands, like Bob Wills and his Texas Playboys and Milton Brown and his Musical Brownies, resent being called "country," a term that they still equate with hillbilly. Western swing bands were dance orchestras, if you please, and some, like Wills and his Playboys, carried as many as forty instruments at a time. Nonetheless, the audiences for western swing dances were country audiences, and it is as country musicians that these players are remembered.

Western swing music does draw from country music for much of its instrumentation, including fiddles and steel guitars. When Bob Wills shouts, "Take it away, Leon!"

he isn't telling steel player Leon MacAuliffe to lay about with the vibraphone. In addition, western swing songs have country lyrics— many of them are about home and work and honky tonking. What really sets this music off from mainstream country is its rhythms, derived mainly from New Orleans jazz rhythms of the twenties and thirties.

Bob Wills is considered to be the father of western swing, and he and his Playboys were indeed the best-known of many bands that traveled the circuit west of the Mississippi in the thirties and forties. There were other fine bands, however, including the one led by Wills's brother Johnny Lee, the aforementioned Milton Brown and his Musical Brownies, and Spade Cooley. Western swing experienced a sharp decline in popularity in the fifties and sixties, and by the time young musicians like Asleep at the Wheel revived it, western swing was considered to be a charming antique.

Freddy Fender, who sings in what might be called a Tex-Mex country style, talks with Ronee Blakley, star of Nashville.

WHO'S ON FIRST?

Most people think that the sound of a steel guitar is synonymous with the sound of country music. Interestingly enough, the steel guitar wasn't even heard on a country music record until 1954—although it had been used in live performances since the early 1940s. The Grand Ole Opry wasn't radio's first "barn dance" show either, and the first female country singer to sell a million records did so fifteen years before Kitty Wells's first hit, "It Wasn't God Who Made Honky Tonk Angels." In the interest of setting the record straight, here's a year-by-year account of country music "firsts." Some of them may surprise you.

1900: Douglas Green, author of *Country Roots*, says that the first printed use of the word "hillbillie" occurred in the April 23, 1900, edition of the *New York Journal.*

1922: "Uncle" Eck Robertson and Henry Gilliand traveled to New York, where they recorded what is generally considered to be the first country music record, for Victor on June 30. Both songs recorded were fiddle tunes—"Sallie Goodin" and "The Arkansas Traveller." Although most of the best fiddle players of the time came from the Southeast, Uncle Eck was born in Amarillo, Texas.

On August 14, 1922, the Jenkins Family, a gospel group from Georgia, became the first "old time" musicians to broadcast on radio. They appeared on Atlanta station WSB.

1923: Fiddlin' John Carson's "Little Old Log Cabin in the Lane," recorded by Ralph Peer on June 14 in Atlanta, is considered to be country music's first hit record. Although the Robertson/Gilliand recordings were made earlier than Carson's, they weren't released until after Carson's record proved that country music records could sell.

On January 4, 1923, WBAP Radio in Fort Worth, Texas, broadcast the first radio "barn dance" show.

1924: "The Prisoner's Song," backed with "The Wreck of the Old 97," recorded August 13 by Vernon Dalhart, was the first country music record ever to sell a million copies. Technically, Dalhart (whose real name was Marion Try Slaughter) was the first singer to change from pop to country, since he had specialized in light opera and parlor songs before recording "The Prisoner's Song."

On April 19, 1924, WLS Radio in Chicago broadcast the debut of the "Chicago Barn Dance," which went on to become the highly popular "National Barn Dance." The show, which broadcast continuously until May, 1960, launched such stars as Gene Autry, Red Foley, George Gobel, Grandpa and Ramona Jones, Bradley Kincaid, and the Coon Creek Girls.

On July 8, Uncle Dave Macon made his first records in New York. Working with Sid Harkreader on guitar, Uncle Dave recorded "Keep My Skillet Good and Greasy," "Hill Billie Blues," and "Fox Hunt."

1925: On November 28 the "WSM Barn Dance," which later became "Grand Ole Opry," first broadcast from WSM's Studio A in Nashville. The first person to perform on the show was fiddler Uncle Jimmy Thompson, accompanied by his niece, Mrs. Eva Thompson Jones, on piano.

Deford Bailey, "the harmonica wizard," was the first black to perform on the Opry program. He first appeared shortly after the show began and remained as a featured performer until 1941.

Uncle Dave Macon, "the Dixie Dewdrop," began appearing on the barn dance during its first year. His performances became more and more frequent as the years went by, and he is credited with being the Opry's first star. With his band, the Fruit Jar Drinkers, Uncle Dave stayed with the Opry until his death in 1952, at the age of 82.

1927: The name "Grand Ole Opry" was coined in December by master of ceremonies George D. Hay, "the Solemn Old Judge."

In August 1927, both the Carter Family and Jimmie Rodgers made their first rec-ords for Ralph Peer of Victor, in Bristol, Tennessee/Virginia (the town sits on the border of the two states). The Carters recorded "Bury Me Beneath the Willow" and three other songs. Rodgers made "The Soldier's Sweetheart," backed with "Rock All Our Babies to Sleep." These sessions mark the beginnings of commercial country music.

The East Texas Serenaders—a protowestern swing band—made its first records for Brunswick during this year. The band, composed of fiddler D. H. Williams, tenor banjoist John McMunnerlin, guitarist Claude Hammonds, and cellist Henry Bogan, was influential in the development of swing musicians like Bob Wills and Milton Brown.

1928: Technically, the first record ever made in Nashville was a Victor field recording of early Opry string bands, made on September 28. The real start of regular recording in Nashville did not begin until 1945.

1929: Gene Autry, who would become America's most popular "Singing Cowboy," made his first record on October 9.

The Singing Brakeman, starring Jimmie Rodgers, was made in this year; it is probably the first "country music movie" ever made. The fifteen-minute short can now be seen at the Country Music Hall of Fame in Nashville.

1930: Ken Maynard, starring in *Song of the Saddle,* was Hollywood's first singing cowboy.

Clockwise: Vernon Dalhart, country's first million-selling singer; Uncle Jimmy Thompson, whose fiddling opened the first broadcast of the "WSM Barn Dance"—later to become the Grand Ole Opry; Deford Bailey, one of the Opry's earliest featured performers and its first black cast member; Pee Wee King and his Golden West Cowboys, who were among the first country entertainers to adopt western dress.

Clockwise: *Uncle Dave Macon, "the Dixie Dewdrop," was the most popular of the early Opry stars. Hank Williams made his first record in 1946. Bob Wills, "the King of Western Swing," formed the Texas Playboys in 1933.*

Sheldon and Goldblatt, in *The Country Music Story*, state that this is also the year that musicians first began appearing on the Opry wearing western clothes, citing Ken Hackley's band as the pioneers. (Pee Wee King and his Golden West Cowboys, who joined the Opry in 1936, are traditionally credited with inaugurating this style.)

Dr. J. R. Brinkley, the infamous "goat gland doctor," began broadcasting country music from radio station XERA in Villa Acuna, Mexico, just across the border from Del Rio, Texas. The Carter Family and Jimmie Rodgers worked for XERA during the decade and spread country music to the West Coast via the migrants who left Oklahoma's Dust Bowl for California.

1931: Tex Ritter appeared in *Green Grow the Lilacs* on Broadway, thus becoming the first country music star ever to appear on the Great White Way.

1932: The first of the Grand Ole Opry's "Picnics," or traveling shows, was held in West Tennessee. The crowd was said to have numbered 8,000 people.

1933: The first female stars of the "Grand Ole Opry" (not counting Mrs. Eva Thompson Jones) were Mrs. Edna Wilson and Mrs. Margaret Waters, who performed on the show as "Sarie and Sally."

Bob Wills formed his Texas Playboys (originally Bob Wills and the Playboys), the band that would become the definitive western swing band in America.

WWVA Radio of Wheeling, West Virginia, began the "WWVA Jamboree," which can still be heard every Saturday night, and WLS's "National Barn Dance" joined NBC's Blue Network, the first country barn dance show to be aired nationally.

The Sons of the Pioneers, the most influential of California's singing cowboy bands,

was formed, starring Bob Nolan and Leonard Slye (Roy Rogers). This is still considered to be the best cowboy band ever to record.

1934: Gene Autry's first movie role was a cameo in Ken Maynard's *In Old Santa Fe*. The former star of the National Barn Dance was so well received that later in the same year he got his own starring role, as a singing sci-fi cowboy in *The Phantom Empire*. Autry became the country's most popular singing movie cowboy.

1935: On August 16 Patsy Montana recorded "I Want to Be a Cowboy's Sweetheart," the first country record by a female singer to sell a million copies.

Bob Wills and his Texas Playboys made their first records on September 23.

This is probably the year during which jukeboxes were introduced to truck stops and restaurants in the South. The jukeboxes had a profound effect on the kinds of music that country stars recorded, and helped influence the development of the honky tonk style.

1936: The first use of the term honky tonk in a song title is believed to have been in Al Dexter's "Honky Tonk Blues," recorded in this year.

Roy Acuff made his first recordings—"Wabash Cannon Ball" and "The Great Speckled Bird"—on October 26.

Ernest Tubb also made his first records during this year.

1937: John Lair's "Renfro Valley Barn Dance" was first broadcast from station WLW in Cincinnati. The show, which starred many ex-members of the "National Barn Dance," later moved to Renfro Valley, Kentucky, and can still be seen every Saturday night.

1939: Red River Dave sang his composition "The Ballad of Amelia Earhart" on television, from the RCA Pavilion at the 1939

Left: *Maybelle Carter, "the Mother of Country Music," was an influence on generations of performers who followed her.* Below: *the Grand Ole Opry moved to the famous Ryman Auditorium, "the Mother Church of Country Music," in 1941.* Far right: *Patsy Montana with her million-selling song.*

World's Fair in New York, and proclaimed himself to be "the world's first television star."

The first film about the Grand Ole Opry—entitled *Grand Ole Opry*—was made in Hollywood and starred Roy Acuff and Uncle Dave Macon.

In October Bill Monroe made his first appearance on the Opry stage, singing "Muleskinner Blues," giving birth to bluegrass music.

The Opry's Prince Albert Tobacco segment was first broadcast on national radio.

1940: Clell Summey, of Pee Wee King's Golden West Cowboys, played the electric guitar on the Opry stage, claiming to be the first musician to do so—the record is also claimed by Sam McGee and Paul Howard.

1941: Pop star Bing Crosby recorded "You Are My Sunshine" and "New San Antonio Rose," both of which became hits. These were probably the first country "crossover" songs—meaning that they were popular with a national, not just country, audience.

This is also considered to be the year when an electric guitar was first used on a country music record. According to the story, jukebox operators complained to Ernest Tubb that his records could not be heard over the din of their noisy honky tonks. Tubb proceeded to employ Fay (Smitty) Smith, staff guitarist for KGKO in Fort Worth, to play electric guitar on one of his recording sessions in 1941. Later, Jimmie Short, Tubb's regular

guitarist, is said to have attached an electrical pickup to his guitar for live performances.

1942: Elton Britt's "There's a Star-Spangled Banner Waving Somewhere," a song about a crippled boy who wants to help with the war effort, was country music's first gold record. Britt's award came from his record company, but later, a trade association—the Recording Industry Association of America (RIAA)—began to audit record sales, awarding gold records to any disks that generated a million dollars in sales. Britt's record is said to have sold several million copies.

1943: Fred Rose and Roy Acuff formed Acuff-Rose, the first song publishing firm in Nashville, which became an outlet for songwriters like Hank Williams, who probably could not have obtained songwriting contracts elsewhere in the country.

1944: *Billboard*, the music industry's leading trade publication, introduced the first country music popularity charts, under the heading "Most Played Juke Box Folk Records," a step that further legitimized the country music business.

1945: Red Foley recorded at WSM's Studio B in Nashville in March or April of this year, and is considered to be the first person to record officially in Nashville, aside from the 1928 Victor field recordings. The real start of commercial recording in Nashville is said to have occurred on September 11, when Ernest Tubb made "It Just Don't Matter Now" and "When Love Turns to Hate," under the direction of Decca's Paul Cohen, who was Nashville's first major producer.

1946: Hank Williams made his first record for the Sterling label, on December 11.

1947: On September 18 and 19 the first country music show ever to be presented at

New York City's Carnegie Hall was headlined by Ernest Tubb and Roy Acuff, and people had to be turned away from the doors.

Harold "Sticks" McDonald, of Pee Wee King's Golden West Cowboys, claims to have been the first person to play drums on the stage of the "Grand Ole Opry" during this year. The claim is disputed by Smokey Dacus, drummer for Bob Wills and his Texas Playboys, who says that he played drums at the Opry in 1946—behind the curtains. Even today, nothing more than a simple set of snare drums is allowed on the Opry stage.

1948: The first country music show to be broadcast regularly by television was "Midwestern Hayride," which debuted on WLW from Cincinnati on January 13.

1949: The trade magazine *Billboard* changed the name of its country music popularity charts from "Most Played Juke Box Folk Records" to "Country and Western," thus legitimizing the term in the business. (Black music charts were renamed "Rhythm and Blues" at about the same time.)

Hank Williams made his first appearance on the "Grand Ole Opry," singing "Lovesick Blues."

1950: Hank Snow made his first appearance on the "Grand Ole Opry" on January 7. On September 30, the Opry was broadcast by television for the first time.

1951: Pop singers Patti Page and Tony Bennett recorded "Tennessee Waltz" and "Cold, Cold Heart," respectively, and achieved mass popularity for country songs for the first

---

Johnny Cash and Elvis Presley began recording—and revolutionizing—country music in the mid-fifties.

time since 1941. The Bennett recording was Hank Williams' first crossover hit and did much to make Hank's name known nationally.

1952: Eddy Arnold, "the Tennessee Plowboy," became the first country star to host a network television show, when he was chosen to be Perry Como's summer replacement on NBC-TV.

1953: Bill Haley's Saddle Pals released "Crazy, Man, Crazy" under the name Bill Haley and the Comets, thus becoming the first country band to switch to rock and roll.

1954: The pedal steel guitar was first used on record, played by Bud Isaacs on Webb Pierce's "Slowly."

Elvis Presley's first recording session took place at Sun studios in Memphis on July 19.

1955: George Jones had his first hit record—"Why Baby Why?"

Johnny Cash made his first recordings for Sun.

1956: The first rock and roll sessions in Nashville were held in January. Elvis Presley, newly signed to RCA, came first and recorded his first RCA release, "Heartbreak Hotel." Twenty days later (January 20), Buddy Holly cut "Blue Days Black Nights," backed with "Love Me," with Decca's Owen Bradley producing (the record was released in April). Both Holly and Presley cut several other songs during these sessions. Presley's were all immediately successful, but Holly's were not hits until much later. The latter's Nashville recordings are available as an import from MCA in Great Britain, under the title *Buddy Holly: The Nashville Sessions.*

1957: The Country Music Association, the first country music trade organization, was formed.

1958: The Kingston Trio's recording of "Tom Dooley" won the first country music Grammy award. The Trio's growing popularity was an early signal that rockabilly was already entering a decline, and "Tom Dooley" helped spark the folk music revival of the early sixties.

1960: The first Loretta Lynn record to make the country music charts was "Honky Tonk Girl," which entered *Billboard*'s charts on June 19.

1961: On November 3 Fred Rose, Hank Williams, and Jimmie Rodgers were installed as the first members of the Country Music Hall of Fame.

On December 13 Jimmy Dean's album *Big Bad John* became the first country music record to receive the gold certification (signifying sales of a million dollars) from the Recording Industry Association of America. Tennessee Ernie Ford's *Hymns* won the gold certification in 1959 as a gospel record.

1962: On November 9 Roy Acuff was announced as the first living member of the Country Music Hall of Fame.

On May 26 Willie Nelson's "Touch Me" entered the country popularity charts, the first of his records to do so.

1964: Johnny Cash cut "It Ain't Me, Babe," becoming the first country singer to cut a Bob Dylan song—an enterprise that would reach fruition with *Nashville Skyline* in 1969.

1966: Bob Dylan was the first of the new generation of rock singers to cut a major album in Nashville. It was called *Blonde on Blonde.*

1967: This was the year of the first country rock album—*Safe At Home* by the

International Submarine Band, featuring Gram Parsons. Parsons joined the Byrds shortly thereafter, and the group produced *Sweetheart of the Rodeo*, one of the better-known early L.A. country rock albums, the next year.

The first Country Music Association Awards show was held in October.

1969: *Hee Haw*, the popular syndicated country television show, made its debut.

1970: Ringo Starr was the first Beatle to record in Nashville. Paul McCartney followed suit later, recording with Chet Atkins.

1971: The first annual Fan Fair was held in Nashville's Municipal Auditorium.

1972: The first Dripping Springs, Texas, "Picnic" was held in March. Willie Nelson appeared on the three-day outdoor show,

but he did not begin sponsoring the picnics until the next year. The original redneck-meets-hippie festival was organized by a group of Dallas businessmen.

Loretta Lynn was elected the Country Music Association's "Entertainer of the Year," the first woman to be so honored.

1973: Willie Nelson sponsored his first "Fourth of July Picnic," at Dripping Springs, Texas. This event heralded the beginning of outlaw music's dominance of country music.

The Opryland amusement park (but not the Opry itself) opened for business.

Meanwhile, on the stage of the old Ryman Auditorium, Kinky Friedman and the Texas Jewboys, appearing on the "Grand Ole Gospel Show," were announced to be the "first full-blooded Jews" to appear on the Opry stage. The Reverend Jimmy Snow, Hank Snow's son, said so.

Patsy Cline was the first female solo per-

Dobie Gray, Reverend Jimmy Snow, Jewford Shelby, Kinky Friedman, Billy Swan, and Willie Fong Young on the stage of the Grand Ole Opry, 1973.

WILLIE NELSON'S
4TH of JULY PICNIC

WAYLON JENNINGS · TOM T. HALL
RITA COOLIDGE · KRIS KRISTOFFERSON
DOUG SAHM · SAMMIE SMITH

AT

PLUS MANY MORE...

DRIPPING FROM HIGHWAY 71 TAKE HIGHWAY 290 WEST THRU DRIPPING SPRINGS THEN FOLLOW THE SIGNS **SPRINGS**

Wanted: The Outlaws *was country's first platinum record. Here, Tompall, Waylon, Jessi, and Willie get their awards from RCA's Chet Atkins, Jerry Bradley, and Ken Glancy.*

former to be elected to the Country Music Hall of Fame.

1974: The Grand Ole Opry's first show at the new Opry House, on the grounds of Opryland, U.S.A., took place on March 16. Richard M. Nixon was a surprise guest and is so far the only U.S. President ever to have appeared on the Opry. Nixon learned yo-yo tricks from Roy Acuff and joined the cast in singing "Will the Circle Be Unbroken?"

George Hamilton IV toured the Soviet Union, the first country performer to do so.

1976: *Wanted: The Outlaws,* an RCA album featuring Waylon Jennings, Willie Nelson, Jessi Colter, and Tompall Glaser, was the first country music record to be awarded the platinum designation (signifying sales of 1,000,000 copies) by the RIAA. Several other country albums probably sold a million copies before *The Outlaws*, but the RIAA had no platinum award at the time.

1979:
Willie Nelson made his film debut—as Robert Redford's manager in *The Electric Horseman*—on December 21.

1980:
Jimmy Carter became the first U.S. President to sing a duet with Willie Nelson.

Carter joined Willie in "Amazing Grace" in a Maryland concert during the 1980 Presidential campaign.

Barbara Mandrell and sisters Louise and Irlene became the first female country singers to host a regularly scheduled network television show.

Dolly Parton made her film debut in *Nine to Five*.

MUSICAL FAMILIES

COUNTRY MUSIC'S FIRST FAMILY

Sometimes it seems as if everyone in Nashville is related. That's because, traditionally, country music has been a family business. Many of the more successful duet acts—Wilma Lee and Stoney Cooper, Lulu-Belle and Scotty Wiseman, Carl and Pearl Butler—were husband and wife. There have been brother acts, sister acts, and entire family acts, like the Stonemans, or, today, the Mandrells. The most complicated of these musical families, however, is the Carter Family and its descendants, which, through marriage, childbirth, divorce, and remarriage, has spawned a Gordian knot of relationships. In one case a family member became his own son's uncle.

It began in 1915, when Alvin Pleasant "A. P." Carter married Sara Dougherty of Maces Springs, Virginia. Eleven years later, in 1926, A. P.'s brother Ezra married Sara Dougherty's first cousin Maybelle Addington. The two couples settled near Maces Springs, in a community called Poor Valley. There, A. P., Sara, and Maybelle formed the "original" Carter Family, one of country music's first commercial and most influential groups. In August 1927, Maybelle, A. P., and Sara recorded for Ralph Peer, a scout for Victor Records, in Bristol, Virginia/Tennessee, and country music history was made. During the next seventeen years, the Carter Family recorded about 250 songs on a dozen labels and sold millions of records. Meanwhile, A. P. and Sara had three children, Joe, Gladys, and Jeannette, before divorcing in 1932. Maybelle and Ezra had three daughters, Helen, Anita, and June. Because of the kinships between the parents, the children of the Carter Family were first cousins to each other and first cousins once removed from their respective aunts. Sara Carter married Coy Bayes, A. P. Carter's first cousin, in 1939, and in 1943 the original Carter Family broke up.

Although the Carter Family's successful

Left: *A. P., Sarah, and Maybelle Carter, the founders of country music's First Family.*
Below: *Johnny Cash with his first wife, Vivian Liberto, and daughters Rosanne (with guitar) and Kathy, at home in California.* Right: *June Carter Cash with her eldest daughter, Carlene, whose father is singer Carl Smith.*
Below right: *Rosanne Cash, Johnny's oldest, is following in her father's footsteps. So far, she's made three successful albums.*

merging of mountain folk music with the melodic and commercial instrumental style that Maybelle developed would prove to be a major influence on the styles of many performers to come, the first family never made it to Nashville's Grand Ole Opry, the power center of the business. When the first group broke up, "Mother" Maybelle took Helen, June, and Anita on the road as the "Second Carter Family," and, after working in North Carolina and Richmond, Virginia, made it to the Grand Ole Opry, thus establishing a physical, as well as a musical, presence in the business.

In Nashville, June married singer Carl Smith, who had a popular television show based in Toronto, Ontario. The couple had one daughter, Rebecca Carlene, before divorcing. June then married Madisonville, Tennessee, building contractor Rip Nix. They had a daughter, Rozanne. By this time the Carter Family was touring with Johnny Cash's road show. Cash, who'd married Vivian Liberto in Germany in 1953, had four daughters, Rosanne, Cindy, Kathy, and Tara. Both Cash and June Carter divorced their current spouses, and the two singers married in 1968. All the respective daughters moved in with Cash and Carter, thus becoming step-sisters (except for Carlene Smith and Rosie Nix, who already were half-sisters). Johnny and June proceeded to have a son, John Carter Cash, who became a half-brother to everybody. This is where things began to get complicated.

Carlene was the first of the daughters to marry, at age 15. She had one daughter, Tiffany, before divorcing Joe Simpkins to marry songwriter Jack Ruth. Carlene (who by now was calling herself Carlene Carter) had one son, John Jackson Ruth, before divorcing Jack Ruth. She then dated the songwriter and member of Emmylou Harris' Hot Band Rodney Crowell before going to England, where she met Graham Parker's band, Rumour, and made her first album, released in the United States by Warner Brothers.

Step-sister Rosanne Cash, meanwhile, also went to Europe. Although she was primarily interested in acting at the time, Rosanne made one album for the West German-based Ariola label before returning to the United States and Los Angeles to study acting. There, she began dating Rodney Crowell, who had one daughter, Hannah, by a previous marriage. Rodney and Rosanne married, and each signed solo recording contracts, Rodney with Warner Brothers and Rosanne with Columbia. Albums from both were well received critically, and Rosanne's second record, *Seven-Year Ache,* sold enough copies to win a gold album award certified by the Record Industry Association of America.

In England, Carlene Carter met Nick Lowe, founder of Rockpile, and producer of New Wave singer Elvis Costello. The two were married in 1980, and Lowe produced Carlene's second album. By this time, Rodney Crowell and Rosanne Cash had had a daughter, Caitlin Rivers Crowell. In 1982, the couple had a second daughter, Chelsea Jane.

Back in Nashville, Jack Ruth, Carlene Carter's ex-husband, married Rosanne Cash's sister, Cindy, thus becoming his own son's step-uncle. Fortunately, the couple was divorced before the situation could get any more complicated.

In 1980 Johnny Cash was elected to the Country Music Hall of Fame. His in-laws, the Carter Family, had been elected to the Hall of Fame in 1970. Thus, one of the pioneer families in country music can boast of four members of the Country Music Hall of Fame, and at least six descendants, by birth or marriage, who are actively engaged in the music business fifty-five years after the original family began singing professionally. That's why the Carters are called, justifiably, "the First Family of Country Music."

Here's how their family tree looks:

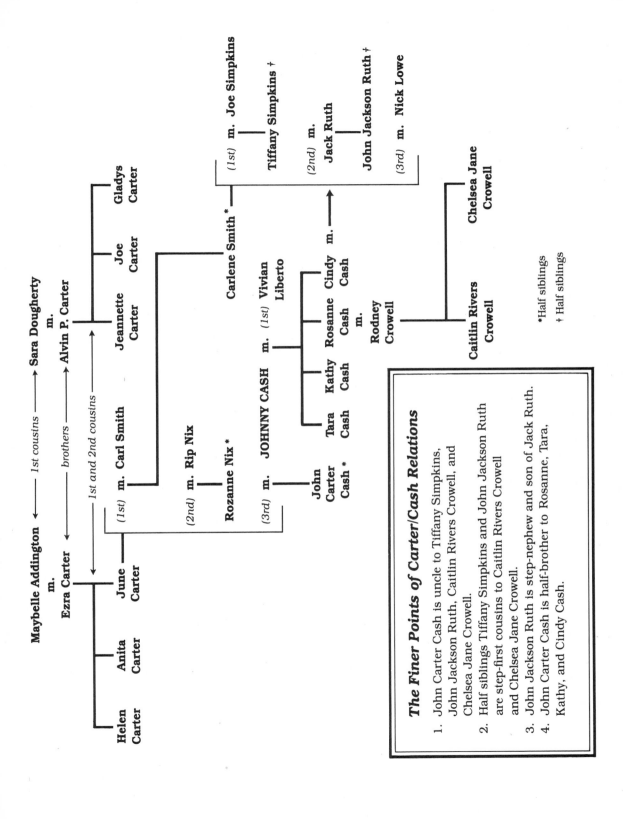

Maybelle Addington
m.
Ezra Carter

← 1st cousins →

→ Sara Dougherty
→ Alvin P. Carter

brothers

1st and 2nd cousins

Helen Carter

Anita Carter

June Carter

Gladys Carter

Joe Carter

Jeannette Carter

(1st) m. Carl Smith

(2nd) m. Rip Nix

Rozanne Nix *

(3rd) m. JOHNNY CASH

John Carter Cash *

Carlene Smith *

m. (1st) Vivian Liberto

Tara Cash

Kathy Cash

Rosanne Cash

Cindy Cash m.

Rodney Crowell

(1st) m. Joe Simpkins

Tiffany Simpkins †

(2nd) m. Jack Ruth

John Jackson Ruth †

(3rd) m. Nick Lowe

Caitlin Rivers Crowell

Chelsea Jane Crowell

*Half siblings
† Half siblings

The Finer Points of Carter/Cash Relations

1. John Carter Cash is uncle to Tiffany Simpkins, John Jackson Ruth, Caitlin Rivers Crowell, and Chelsea Jane Crowell.

2. Half siblings Tiffany Simpkins and John Jackson Ruth are step-first cousins to Caitlin Rivers Crowell and Chelsea Jane Crowell.

3. John Jackson Ruth is step-nephew and son of Jack Ruth.

4. John Carter Cash is half-brother to Rosanne, Tara, Kathy, and Cindy Cash.

TRACING THE HISTORY OF COUNTRY MUSIC THROUGH THE MARRIAGES OF TAMMY WYNETTE

Although the Carter Family tree is historic as well as complicated, singer Tammy Wynette is a one-woman course in country music history. Solely on the basis of the men she's married, one way or another, Tammy can trace her musical pedigree through every major style of country music, with the exception of western swing.

Born Wynette Pugh near Tupelo, Mississippi, in 1942, Tammy's first marriage, to high school sweetheart Euple Byrd, didn't really further her musical career, although it did give her the interesting name of Wynette Pugh Byrd, and three daughters, Jackie, Tina, and Gwen. When her first marriage broke up, Tammy, now equipped with an Alabama beauty operator's license, moved to Birmingham, Alabama, where she worked as a beautician and began singing on the "Country Boy Eddie Show" on WBRC-TV. After doing some club dates and winning a couple of appearances on Porter Wagoner's syndicated show, she decided to strike out for Nashville and stardom.

There, in relatively short order, she changed her name to Tammy Wynette, recorded a hit single, "Apartment Number 9," in 1967, and married songwriter Don Chappel.

Don Chappel's real name is Amburgey, and he's a member of a musical family from Neon, Kentucky, which includes his sisters: Jean Chappel, who was successful in the forties, and Martha Carson, the premier female gospel singer of the late forties. Martha Carson and her ex-husband, James Carson (whose real name is James Roberts), were a highly popular duet act on radio station WSB in Atlanta. Roberts' father,

Fiddlin' Dock Roberts, of Madison County, Kentucky, was one of country music's earliest recording stars, having made several sides for the Gennet label, a subsidiary of the Starr Piano Company of Chicago, in the twenties. So, through this marriage, Tammy Wynette is connected to the very beginnings of country music, as well as to the country and gospel styles popular in the thirties and forties.

Opposite: *Tammy Wynette sings "Stand By Your Man," and she has—five times so far.* **Above:** *Tammy with her third husband, George Jones. Their marriage was stormy, but their duets were unsurpassed.*

Tammy's third, and most famous, marriage was to George Jones, in 1968. Although Jones is country music's premier exponent of the honky tonk exhortative singing style made popular by Hank Williams, he also sang for a while under the name Thumper Jones. These records, released on Texas' Starday label, are rockabilly tunes. This gives Tammy Wynette a connection to the form that revolutionized country music, as well as to what it still considered the classic country singing style. It was this style at which she and Jones excelled as a duet act, and as such, the couple was unsurpassed for the six years that they were together. They were divorced in 1975, having had one daughter, Tamala Georgette Jones.

After her divorce from Jones, Tammy, who is of course one of country music's best female solo singers, worked on her own for a few years. Although she didn't marry anyone else right away, she did have some heavy romances with movie star Burt Reynolds and with Rudy Gatlin, brother of Larry Gatlin, and she tells about them in her extremely interesting autobiography, *Stand By Your Man*.

Then Tammy got the bug again and married Nashville businessman Michael Tomlin, who had absolutely nothing to do with the music business. Appropriately, that marriage ended after six weeks, and Tammy soon married George Richey, an old friend of George Jones, and a songwriter in the smoothed-down, middle-of-the-road style of the seventies. Richey helped produce several of Tammy's records in the late seventies and even effected a temporary professional reconciliation between his wife and Jones. His brother, Paul Richey, signed on as Jones's manager, and for a little while, George, Tammy, George, and Paul traveled together. George Richey sometimes played the piano for Jones and Wynette on these shows, causing George Jones to introduce Richey as "my husband-in-law,"

which seems to me a very useful term in describing this country music musical family.

At the moment Tammy's still married to George Richey, and George Jones has dissolved his managerial ties with Paul Richey. The only thing that I can see that might complicate the situation even further is if Tamala Georgette Jones were to grow up and marry John Carter Cash. That would create a situation that not even *Debrett's Peerage* could untangle, because almost everyone in Nashville would be related to almost everyone else one way or another.

FROM COON CREEK
TO EXILE

Another interesting musical family that is still engaged in the business through its descendants began in the early thirties with the Ledford sisters, Lilly May, Rose, Daisy, and Violet, of the Red River Gorge in Kentucky. Lilly May, proficient on both fiddle and banjo, began playing professionally with her brothers, but when they auditioned for John Lair of WLS's "National Barn Dance," Lilly May was singled out; she played as a solo act for a time until Lair got the idea of forming an all-girl string band. Lilly's sisters were summoned, and the Coon Creek Girls became a featured act on the "Barn Dance." Later, with a slightly different lineup, the Coon Creek Girls performed on Lair's "Renfro Valley Barn Dance" in Kentucky.

Lilly May's sister Rose married Cotton Foley of Berea, Kentucky, and eventually dropped out of the group. Cotton is the brother of the late Red Foley, who starred on WLS's "National Barn Dance," the "Renfro Valley Barn Dance,"

the "Grand Ole Opry," and the "Ozark Jubilee" before his death in 1958. Shirley Foley, the daughter of Red and Eva Overstake (who was one of the Girls of the Golden West), married teenage singing idol Pat Boone and moved to California. Their daughter Debbie, also a singer, married Gabriel Ferrer, son of Jose Ferrer, in 1980.

Lilly May Ledford, who married and divorced twice, stayed with the Coon Creek Girls until the group permanently dissolved in the late fifties. Although troubled with severe arthritis, she still performs at the odd folk festival, and she has also conducted old time music seminars at Berea College, near her hometown of Lexington. One of Lilly May's sons, J. C. Pennington, is a founding member of the rock band Exile, which had a million-selling record in 1979 with a song called "Kiss You All Over." At last report, both mother and son, in their different ways, were still going strong.

Lilly May Ledford was a star of the "National Barn Dance" in Chicago. Her son's a star of rock and roll.

COUSINS—
AND THEN SOME

Just about everyone knows that singers Jerry Lee Lewis and Mickey Gilley, and evangelist Jimmy Lee Swaggart, are first cousins. However, if one really looks into the family histories of the Swaggarts, the Gilleys, and the Lewises—as author Nick Tosches did for *Hellfire*, his recently published biography of Jerry Lee Lewis—he'll find that the three men are much, much more than first cousins. They're cousins

about six different ways. Most of the following information is drawn from Tosches' research, which he has generously allowed me to pass on to you.

The family's tangled relations actually began to become complicated in the nineteenth century, when Jerry Lee's and Mickey's grandfather (and Jimmy Lee's great-grandfather), Leroy Lewis, married his first cousin, Arilla Hampton. When first cousins marry, any

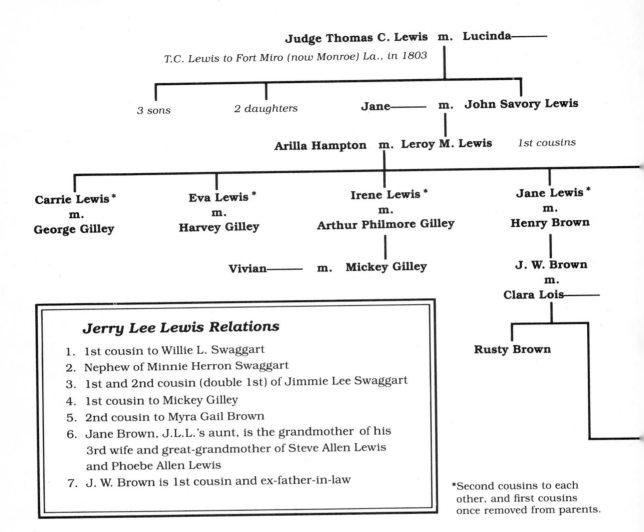

Judge Thomas C. Lewis m. Lucinda——

T.C. Lewis to Fort Miro (now Monroe) La., in 1803

3 sons   *2 daughters*   **Jane—— m. John Savory Lewis**

Arilla Hampton m. Leroy M. Lewis   *1st cousins*

Carrie Lewis *   **Eva Lewis ***   **Irene Lewis ***   **Jane Lewis ***
m.   **m.**   **m.**   **m.**
George Gilley   **Harvey Gilley**   **Arthur Philmore Gilley**   **Henry Brown**

Vivian—— m. Mickey Gilley   **J. W. Brown**
m.
Clara Lois——

Rusty Brown

Jerry Lee Lewis Relations

1. 1st cousin to Willie L. Swaggart
2. Nephew of Minnie Herron Swaggart
3. 1st and 2nd cousin (double 1st) of Jimmie Lee Swaggart
4. 1st cousin to Mickey Gilley
5. 2nd cousin to Myra Gail Brown
6. Jane Brown, J.L.L.'s aunt, is the grandmother of his 3rd wife and great-grandmother of Steve Allen Lewis and Phoebe Allen Lewis
7. J. W. Brown is 1st cousin and ex-father-in-law

*Second cousins to each other, and first cousins once removed from parents.

children they may have become not only brothers and sisters but second cousins to each other and first cousins once removed from their parents.

This was what happened to Leroy's and Arilla's four sons and seven daughters. It became even more complicated when three of the daughters—Carrie, Eva, and Irene—married three Gilley brothers—George, Harvey, and Arthur, respectively—thus becoming, in relation to one another, sisters, second cousins, and sisters-in-law. The children of these couples, would, of course, become double first cousins to one another, since sisters had married brothers, and first cousins twice removed to their maternal grandparents. Mickey Gilley is the son of Irene Lewis Gilley and Arthur P. Gilley.

Meanwhile, Ada Lewis, the daughter of Leroy and Arilla, married Willie Henry Swaggart. They had a son named Willie Leon Swaggart, who married Minnie Bell Herron, the daughter of Theresa Lee Foreman and John William Herron. Minnie Bell's sister, Mary Ethel Herron, called Mamie, married Elmo Lewis, brother of Ada Lewis Swaggart. This made Willie Leon Swaggart the nephew of Elmo Lewis, and

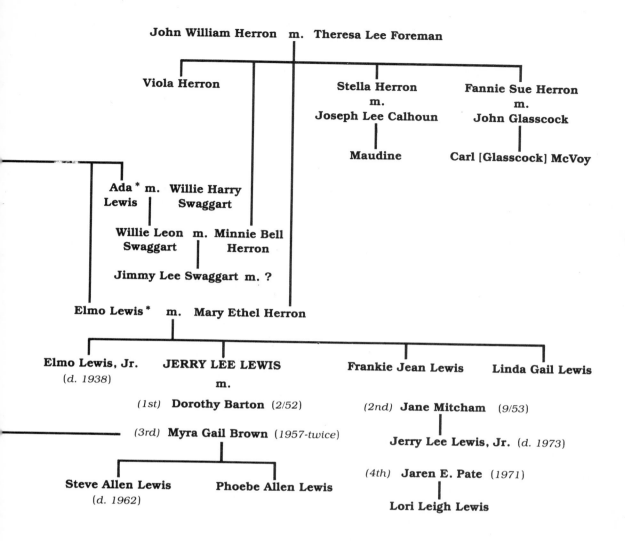

John William Herron m. **Theresa Lee Foreman**

Viola Herron

Stella Herron
m.
Joseph Lee Calhoun

Maudine

Fannie Sue Herron
m.
John Glasscock

Carl [Glasscock] McVoy

Ada * m. **Willie Harry**
Lewis **Swaggart**

Willie Leon m. **Minnie Bell**
Swaggart **Herron**

Jimmy Lee Swaggart m. **?**

Elmo Lewis * m. **Mary Ethel Herron**

Elmo Lewis, Jr. **JERRY LEE LEWIS**
(*d. 1938*) m.

(*1st*) **Dorothy Barton** (*2/52*)

(*3rd*) **Myra Gail Brown** (*1957-twice*)

Steve Allen Lewis **Phoebe Allen Lewis**
(*d. 1962*)

Frankie Jean Lewis **Linda Gail Lewis**

(*2nd*) **Jane Mitcham** (*9/53*)

Jerry Lee Lewis, Jr. (*d. 1973*)

(*4th*) **Jaren E. Pate** (*1971*)

Lori Leigh Lewis

presumably, Willie's wife, Minnie Bell, would have been Elmo's niece, except for the fact that she was the sister of Elmo's wife, Mamie, and so was Elmo's sister-in-law. Thus Elmo was the uncle of Jimmy Lee Swaggart, the son of Willie Leon and Minnie Bell. Since Elmo's wife, Mamie, was Minnie Bell's sister, she was the aunt of Jimmy Lee Swaggart. Therefore, Jerry Lee Lewis, who was Elmo and Mamie's second son, was Jimmy Lee Swaggart's double first cousin, while Mickey Gilley is only a regular first cousin on Jerry Lee's father's side of the family.

The confusion doesn't stop here. Another of Elmo's sisters, Jane Lewis, married Henry Brown. Their son J.W. married a girl named Clara Lois. That couple had two children, Rusty and Myra Gail, who were Jerry Lee's second cousins. After marriages to two women—first Dorothy Barton and then Jane Mitcham, the latter of whom bore Jerry Lee a son named Jerry Lee Lewis, Jr.—Jerry Lee married Myra, his second cousin. This made Jerry Lee's Aunt Jane his grandmother-in-law, and his first cousin, J. W. Brown, his father-in-law. When Jerry Lee and Myra had their two children, Steve Allen Lewis and Phoebe Allen Lewis,

Jerry Lee's Aunt Jane became their great-grandmother, while his first cousin J. W. became the children's grandfather. Moreover, Jerry Lee married Myra twice, thus moving his official total of marriages up to four.

After such prolific marrying, Jerry Lee Lewis' branch of the family dwindled in a tragic manner. Steve Allen Lewis, his son by Myra Brown, died in 1960 when he fell into a swimming pool, and Jerry Lee Lewis, Jr., died in 1973 in a car accident. That left Jerry Lee with only one child, Phoebe Allen Lewis, until he married for a fifth time, to Jaren E. Pate. Jaren bore Jerry Lee one more child, Lori Leigh Lewis, before the couple finally divorced in the late seventies. Since Jerry Lee's brother, Elmo Lewis, Jr., had been killed in a car accident as a child, Elmo Lewis, Sr.'s line will die with Jerry Lee, assuming that the Killer doesn't marry yet again and father a son. It wouldn't be surprising if that were to happen.

Jerry Lee Lewis, whose family tree looks like an experiment in recombinant DNA. Inset: Jerry Lee's double first cousin Mickey Gilley. His mother was one of three sisters who married three brothers.

NAMES

Despite all the fuss about country music being "real" and "downhome" and "honest," it's always contained elements of show business. There's hardly a country performer alive, for example, who hasn't at least considered trading his or her real name for a more catchy stage name. In fact, the very first country record ever to sell a million copies was recorded in 1924 by a Texan who called himself Vernon Dalhart. Dalhart's real name was Marion Try Slaughter, and he took his stage name (one of many that Slaughter used in his career) from the names of two towns in his native Texas.

Early country stage names usually were designed to give audiences some idea of a performer's identity or image. Singing cowboys and cowgirls, such as Montana Slim and Patsy Montana (real names: Wilf Carter and Rubye Blevins), tried to convey their stage images through names and clothes. In the rural Southeast, performers often adopted "family" names to emphasize their connection with the folks. Bashful Brother Oswald (Beecher Kirby) got his name when audiences seemed to object to Roy Acuff's inclusion of a single woman, Rachel Veach, in his traveling show. So Acuff changed her name to Cousin Rachel, enlisted Kirby to be her Bashful (but protective) Brother, and all was well.

Modern country singers change their names not only to ensure a catchy, memorable moniker, but also to reflect the predominantly Anglo-Saxon origins of their audiences. John Denver, for example, was born John Henry Deutschendorf. Not only is Deutschendorf a difficult name to remember, it's also quite German, and therefore not a suitable country music name. Other ethnic names that seem to be out are those derived from Southern and Eastern European roots. There has never been a country singer with an Italian-sounding name, and with the exception of Johnny Rodriguez (John Raul Davis Rodriguez), Spanish names are not represented either.

Finally, there are several out-and-out "gimmick" names. Conway Twitty (Harold Jenkins) got his names from the towns of Conway, Arkansas, and Twitty, Texas. Crystal Gayle (Brenda Gail Webb) was given her name by her sister, Loretta Lynn, who picked it after seeing a spanking white Krystal hamburger stand. Loretta says she picked the name because it's "shiny." Here are more stage names and real names:

Martha Carson	Martha Amburgey
Don and Jean Chapel	Don and Jean Amburgey
Patsy Cline	Virginia Patterson Hensley
Jessi Colter	Miriam Johnson
Danny Davis	George Rowlin
Skeeter Davis	Mary Frances Penick
Jimmy Dean	Seth Ward
Dale Evans	Frances Smith
Donna Fargo	Yvonne Vaughn
Freddy Fender	Baldemar Huerta
Red Foley	Clyde Julian Foley
Tennessee Ernie Ford	Ernest Jennings Ford
Bobbi Gentry	Roberta Streeter
Buddy Holly	James Hardin Holley
Sonny James	Jimmy Loden
Grandpa Jones	Louis Marshall Jones
Pee Wee King	Frank Anthony Kuchinsky
LaCosta	LaCosta Tucker
Brenda Lee	Brenda Mae Tarpley
LuluBelle	Myrtle Cooper Wiseman
Rose Maddox	Rosea Arbana Bragdon
C. W. McCall	William Fries
Molly O'Day	LaVerne Williamson
Buck Owens	Alvis Edgar Owens
Gram Parsons	Cecil Connor
Les Paul	Lester William Polfus
Johnny Paycheck	Donald Lytle
Minnie Pearl	Sarah Ophelia Colley Cannon
Jerry Reed	Jerry Hubbard
Tex Ritter	Maurice Woodward Ritter
Roy Rogers	Leonard Slye
T. G. Sheppard	Bill Browder
Cal Smith	Calvin Grant Shofner
Ray Stevens	Ray Ragsdale
Stringbean	David Akeman
T. Texas Tyler	David Luke Myrick
Doc Watson	Arthel Watson
Kitty Wells	Muriel Deason
Slim Whitman	Otis Dewey
Hank Williams	Hiram Williams
Tammy Wynette	Wynette Pugh

Clockwise: *Loretta Lynn, "the Coal Miner's Daughter"; Crystal Gayle, who got her name from a hamburger stand; Tammy Wynette, née Wynette Pugh; Johnny Paycheck, whose real name is Donald Lytle; Hawkshaw Hawkins, "the Hawk of the West Virginia Hills."*

NICKNAMES

Many country music stars have nicknames in addition to stage names. Usually, the nicknames serve as a kind of shorthand for the audience, either reminding them of the singer's most famous song—as in Loretta Lynn, the Coal Miner's Daughter—or stressing some quality the performer wishes to purvey. If you go to see Jerry Reed, the Alabama Wild Man, you're not going to expect to be lulled to sleep during the show.

Sometimes, entertainers get so famous that they are given titles. Thus Jimmie Rodgers, originally called the Singing Brakeman, or America's Blue Yodeler, is now called the Father of Country Music. Maybelle Carter is the Mother. Kitty Wells and Roy Acuff are, respectively, the Queen and King, while Tammy Wynette serves as the less imperial First Lady.

If a fan knows a singer's nickname, he'll already know a lot about the performer. Envision the people behind these nicknames:

Bill Anderson	Whispering Bill
Eddy Arnold	The Tennessee Plowboy
Chet Atkins	Mr. Guitar
Elton Britt	The World's Greatest Yodeler
Archie Campbell	The Mayor of Bull's Gap
Johnny Cash	The Man in Black
Jerry Clower	The Mouth of the Mississippi
David Allan Coe	The Mysterious Rhinestone Cowboy
Cowboy Copas	The Waltz King of the Grand Ole Opry
Donna Fargo	The Happiest Girl in the U.S.A.
Jack Greene	The Jolly Giant
Merle Haggard	Hag, or the Stranger
Tom T. Hall	The Storyteller
Hawkshaw Hawkins	The Hawk of the West Virginia Hills

George D. Hay	The Solemn Ole Judge
Johnny Horton	The Singing Fisherman
Sonny James	The Southern Gentleman
George Jones	The Crown Prince of Country Music
Bradley Kincaid	The Kentucky Mountain Boy
Jerry Lee Lewis	The Killer
Uncle Dave Macon	The Dixie Dewdrop
Joe and Rose Lee Maphis	Mr. and Mrs. Country Music
Bill Monroe	The Father of Bluegrass Music
Ray Price	The Cherokee Cowboy
Jerry Reed	The Alabama Wild Man
Jim Reeves	Gentleman Jim
Charlie Rich	The Silver Fox
Roy Rogers	King of the Cowboys
Dorothy Shay	The Park Avenue Hillbilly
Hank Snow	The Singing Ranger
Ernest Tubb	The Texas Troubadour
Conway Twitty	The High Priest of Country Music
Hank Williams	The Drifting Cowboy
Del Wood	Queen of the Ivories
Faron Young	The Singing Sheriff

TRADEMARKS

Some stars emphasize their identities with songs, others with nicknames, and still others with "trademarks," or gimmicks that are associated with their appearances. These don't always work. Kenny Rogers, for example, tried throwing out "Kenny Rogers Frizbees" at his shows; he also gave out buttons that proclaimed "I spent the night with Kenny Rogers" to everyone who attended a concert. Neither one of these items ever became associated with the Kenny Rogers image. Other stars, however, just wouldn't seem complete without his or her special piece of equipment or clothing or whatever. For each "trademark" listed below, supply the name of the star:

A. A red bandana
B. A battered hat
C. A white "Planter's" suit
D. A railroader's hat
E. Dark glasses
F. Silk scarves
G. Black suits
H. Blond wigs
I. Hat with a price tag on it

J. Yo-yo tricks
K. Guitar with "thank you" inscribed on the back
L. Elaborate nudie-designed suits
M. A "tramp" costume
N. "Lone Ranger" mask
O. "Granny" glasses
P. A stammer
Q. Overalls

Elvis Presley with his scarves.

ANSWERS

A. Willie Nelson
B. Don Williams
C. Jerry Clower
D. Jimmie Rodgers
E. Roy Orbison, Ronnie Milsap
F. Elvis Presley
G. Johnny Cash
H. Dolly Parton
I. Minnie Pearl

J. Roy Acuff
K. Ernest Tubb
L. Hank Snow (Porter Wagoner used to be known for the same style)
M. Boxcar Willie
N. Orion
O. Grandpa Jones and John Denver
P. Mel Tillis
Q. Junior Samples

Willie Nelson with his bandana.

THE COUNTRY MUSIC IMAGE

Barring election to the Country Music Hall of Fame, the highest honor a country music star can receive is to be elected the Country Music Association's "Entertainer of the Year." The criteria outlined for voters to follow in making their selection for the award are supposedly the most rigorous possible—the CMA wants its entertainers to be the best.

Therefore, the voter is asked to "give consideration not only to recorded performance, but also to in-person performance, staging, public acceptance, attitude, leadership, and overall contribution to the Country Music image."

Obviously the voter wants to elect someone who's popular, talented, and entertaining, but what in the world is meant by "Country Music image"? Though a definition of the "Country Music image" is not to be found in a book, nor could most country entertainers define it either, such a thing does exist, and people who are familiar with country music are supposed to know what it is without being told. Moreover, the qualities needed in the composition of the Country Music image can be changed from

time to time, and voters are supposed to know when a taboo has been lifted—again without being told.

Johnny Cash, for example, is the current embodiment of the image. His qualifications include: upbringing by poor white Southerners; natural talent; early success followed by difficult times; the conquering of the problems of drug abuse and hard living; marriage into country music's first family; finding God; professing concern for the underdogs of this world; rugged individualism, à la John Wayne; ditto on patriotism; popularity within and without the industry; and a commanding physical presence. He is, of course, a fine performer and recording artist.

And yet, a few years ago, Johnny Cash couldn't have bought the Entertainer of the Year award, because certain of the qualities that work in his favor now would have worked against him then. The drug problem and the wild living might not have disqualified him so long as they were safely in the past, but at one time, Johnny criticized the war in Vietnam and thus criticized our government. This was no way for a country performer, much less an Entertainer of the Year, to have behaved. The Country Music image is a delicate thing indeed.

The best way to explain the nature of this beast is to put it in the form of an interview. Most journalists who specialize in country music tend to ask the same questions of everyone they meet, and the monotony works in our favor, because these questions, and the answers to them, define the Country Music image fairly well.

Here are the dos and don'ts of an interview with the ideal country singer. Each question represents a crucial step in the erection of a perfect Country Music image. Answer incorrectly and you're done for, so pay attention!

Q: What was your childhood/family background like?

A: DO say your family was poor and Southern if at all possible. You had many brothers and sisters, a hard-working daddy, and a mama who tried. (Note: it's possible to have had a ne'er-do-well for a daddy, but never for a mama. Mamas are all perfect.) You heard your first country music at home, either because your parents picked and sang, or because you listened to the radio a lot. You went to church, where you loved the music. You never had much, but you were happy.

DON'T say you came from a comfortable middle-class home with two cars in the garage, and a daddy who worked as an executive in the insurance industry. If this is the case, you'd do better to say as little as possible about it. Be vague. Say something like, "Oh, I grew up just like everybody else did," or better yet, "I don't like to talk about it."

The Country Music image—do this.

Above: Don't *do this!* **Right:** *Barbara Mandrell usually cries when she wins an award—this is very good form.*

Q: How did you get started in music?

A: DO say you loved music ever since you were a child. Say your mama bought you a guitar when you were 10 years old. Say everybody thought you had talent, but it wasn't until you won first prize at the school talent show that you took yourself seriously. You moved to Nashville right after high school and knocked on doors along Music Row without success for several years until (insert any name) discovered you and signed you to a recording contract.

DON'T say you took music lessons or played in your high school band. Don't say your father is the president of XYZ Record Company and gave you a recording contract for your birthday. Don't say you used to be a rock and roll singer and switched to

Doug Sahm didn't do too well as a country star. Can you guess why? Opposite: Willie Nelson poses as a saint; he knows the angles when it comes to images.

country only because rock records weren't selling that year. If this is so, say you played rock and roll only to make a living until you got your big break in country music.

Q: What was your big break?

A: DO say that it's all due to (name any country singer) letting you be on his or her show and giving you a solo part. Say your big break came when you overheard a couple arguing in a honky tonk and were thus inspired to compose your hit song, "The Friday Night Fights." Do thank God, and your fans.

DON'T say you got to be successful because you worked harder than anybody else or because you're smarter and more talented than anyone else. Don't say you planned it.

Q: Who are your biggest influences? Your favorite performers?

A: DO name anyone who's dead or who is over 70 years old. Always include Hank, Jimmie Rodgers, and Lefty Frizzell. If you must name a contemporary as a favorite, don't name anyone in country music—say "Tom Jones" or "John Wayne."

DON'T name any of your competitors. Don't name anyone younger than you. Don't name Mick Jagger, Ted Nugent, or the Sex Pistols. Bob Dylan and the Beatles should be safe to name in a couple more years.

Q: What has been the biggest thrill of your career?

A: DO say it happened when you first set foot on the stage of the Grand Ole Opry.

Also acceptable is the day you first heard your own record on the car radio.

DON'T say it was the day you made your first million dollars, or the day when you paid cash for your first Cadillac.

Q: What's your favorite food/color?

A: DO say "beans and cornbread," "fried chicken," or "chicken fried steak." Colors should be blue, blue, or blue.

DON'T say "pâté de foie gras," or any other food with a foreign name, except chili. Don't say black, brown, or pink. Also avoid mauve, puce, magenta, and any other color with a suspicious-sounding name.

Q: What do you do when you have time off?

A: DO say fishing, horseback riding, gardening (vegetables only), or playing with your kids.

DON'T say gambling, shopping, drinking, playing chess, or reading.

Finally, here is a list of subjects which might come up in an interview and what to do about them:

DO *talk about:* illnesses, Mama, Hank, ESP, diets, gardening, fishing, poverty, your fans (favorable comments only), divorce, your kids, ghosts, any dead country singer, Mama, Mama, and Mama.

DON'T *talk about:* art, politics, gourmet food, college, math, science, world history, economics, high fashion, the ERA, women's lib, abortion, taxes, Communists, Socialists, ethnic groups, welfare, foreign policy, Israel, the Third World, or the United Nations.

COMMON INTERESTS

In each of the following groups, an element of common interest is to be found. In a list of songs, for example, the common thread might be that all were written by the same person. In a list of people, all the members of the group will have shared some life experience. Try to identify the common interest for each.

1. Tammy Wynette, Dinah Shore, and Sally Field.

2. Bradley Kincaid, Red Foley, George Gobel, Gene Autry, and the Coon Creek Girls.

3. Earl Scruggs, Lester Flatt, Jimmy Martin, Carter Stanley, and Kenny Baker.

4. Dolly Parton and Hank Snow.

5. January 1, 1953; November 5, 1960; March 5, 1963; and July 31, 1964.

6. Slim Whitman and Montana Slim.

7. Dolly Parton, Loretta Lynn, Roy Acuff, and Grandpa Jones.

8. Roy Drusky, Roy Acuff, Jim Reeves, and Charley Pride.

9. Euple Byrd, Don Chapell, George Jones, Michael Tomlin, and George Richey.

10. Hank Snow, Montana Slim, Anne Murray, and Bob Nolan.

11. Roy Acuff, Jimmie Davis, LuluBelle Wiseman, and W. Lee O'Daniel.

12. Minnie Pearl, Tex Ritter, Bradley Kincaid, Donna Fargo, Roy Orbison, and Hank Thompson.

13. Hank Thompson, Archie Campbell, Roy Drusky, the Duke of Paducah, and Stonewall Jackson.

14. Dale Evans, Waylon Jennings, Jeannie C. Riley, and Willie Nelson.

15. Merle Haggard, David Allan Coe, and Spade Cooley.

16. "I'm Thinking Tonight of My Blue Eyes," "The Great Speckled Bird," "Wild Side of Life," and "It Wasn't God Who Made Honky Tonk Angels."

ANSWERS

1. All have dated movie actor Burt Reynolds.

2. All were stars of WLS's "National Barn Dance" in Chicago.

3. All have been members of Bill Monroe's Bluegrass Boys.

4. Both wear wigs.

5. Each is the date of death of a famous country star. Hank Williams died January 1, 1953; Johnny Horton died in a car wreck November 5, 1960; Patsy Cline, Randy Hughes, Hawkshaw Hawkins and Cowboy Copas died in a plane crash March 5, 1963; Jim Reeves died in a plane crash July 31, 1964.

6. Both men are noted for their Swiss-style yodeling. Whitman's yodel style is patterned directly after Montana Slim's.

7. None of these people have ever been divorced.

8. All were semi-pro baseball players before becoming country musicians. Acuff almost signed with the New York Giants, but recurring sunstrokes forced him to give up the game. Roy Drusky was a star athlete in high school and was sought by the Cleveland Indians. Jim Reeves pitched for the University of Texas team and played for the St. Louis Cardinals' farm team in Lynchburg, Virginia. Charley Pride played for the Memphis Red Sox and for a New York Mets farm team in Helena, Montana, before becoming a country singer.

9. All were married to Tammy Wynette. George Richey still is:

10. All were born in Canada.

11. All are politicians. Roy Acuff ran for Governor of Tennessee in 1944, 1946, and 1948 on the Republican ticket. Jimmie Davis served two terms as Governor of Louisiana. LuluBelle Wiseman was a North Carolina State Representative. W. Lee O'Daniel parlayed his success with the Light Crust Doughboys into the Governorship of Texas.

12. All are either college graduates or have attended college. Minnie Pearl was graduated from exclusive Ward Belmont College in Nashville. Tex Ritter studied law at the University of Texas and Northwestern University in Chicago. Bradley Kincaid attended Berea College in Kentucky and graduated from the YMCA's college in Chicago. Donna Fargo is a certified high school teacher. Roy Orbison majored in geology at North Texas State College. Hank Thompson attended Princeton University.

13. All served in the United States Navy.

14. All were born in Texas.

15. All served time in the penitentiary.

16. All four songs have the same tune, which was apparently derived from a nineteenth-century song. The Carter Family was the first group to record the tune in 1929.

_____

Opposite: *LuluBelle Wiseman: a career in politics?* **Inset:** *Jim Reeves, a former pro baseball player.*

THE ROADHOG'S RULES
FOR BEING A COUNTRY STAR

In days past, traveling country music shows invariably included a comedian. Sometimes the comedian performed alone—Whitey Ford, "the Duke of Paducah," was one such entertainer, and he was popular enough eventually to have his own national radio show—while other acts featured a comedian in the band, often as the bass player. "Stringbean" (David Akeman) was one of Bill Monroe's Bluegrass Boys for a time; Roy Acuff featured Bashful "Brother" Oswald (Beecher Kirby) on dobro and his "Cousin" Rachel (Veach) in early shows, and later, Acuff featured Cousin Jody (Clell Summey), who played steel guitar and did comedy routines.

The Grand Ole Opry used to feature comedians regularly as part of the show. In addition to the famous Minnie Pearl, one of the first female acts at the Opry was the comedy team of Sarie and Sallie. Lasses and Honey, who performed in blackface, were Opry regulars, as were Rod Brasfield, Grandpa Jones, and Speck Rhodes. But in the fifties country music was moving "uptown," and the rube and blackface jokes of the old comedians just didn't fit the new sophisticated image. Today there are only a few good country comedians left—many of them huddled in the *Hee Haw* ghetto of television. Minnie Pearl still works, as does Jerry Clower, but new comic faces have not entered the country field.

That's why so many people were happy when the Statler Brothers, long one of country's most popular quartets, introduced us to Lester "Roadhog" Moran and his Cadillac Cowboys in 1972, on the album *Country Music Then and Now*. Lester Moran lives in Rainbow Valley, where, during the week, he works at the Hogan County Shoe Factory. On the weekends, however, Lester turns from a "mild-mannered foreman into an Ambassador of Country Music." With his Cadillac Cowboys—Wichita, Red, and Wesley—Lester has a fifteen-minute radio show every Saturday morning on WEAK in Rainbow Valley. And each and every Saturday night, the boys play the big dance at the Johnny Mack Brown High School.

The best comedy exaggerates that with which most people are familiar, and anyone who grew up south of the Mason-Dixon Line can remember at least one band in town whose members longed to become stars of the Grand Ole Opry. These bands always had a Saturday morning radio show, and these bands were always incredibly bad. Lester has recreated this world perfectly, and his shows are a hilarious mix of ineptly played cover versions of country hits interspersed with commercials for Rainbow Valley's captains of commerce. There's Burford of Burford's Barbershop, where you can "get clipped." There's Ernie Cupp of Ernie's Egg Market, who sells cracked eggs half price after seven o'clock, and there's Roy of Roy's Radio Repair, whose slogan is, "If it ain't broke, don't bring it to Roy." Two of these radio shows are available on record, the first on *Country Music Then and Now*, which the Statler Brothers shared with the Cadillac Cowboys, and the second on *Alive at the Johnny Mack Brown High School*, Lester's first—and only—album, which also features a live recording of the Saturday night dance. The boys can also be heard on an out-of-print promotional album in which DJ Ralph Emery interviews both the Cadillac Cowboys and the Statler Brothers. *Alive at the Johnny Mack Brown High School* is quite simply the funniest country music record ever made, and no collection is complete without it.

In 1976 *Country Music Magazine* asked Lester to give the magazine's readers the benefit of his years of experience. What follows is the Old Roadhog's completely uncensored manuscript explaining how to get in good ole country music.

Dear *Country Music Magazine:*

You have asked me to right on how to git in good ole country music to help young people who aint stars yet. It aint easy but then it aint all that hard either. Here are some points that you gotta do to make yourself like Johnny Cash, Hank Snow, Del Reeves and of course yours truly the old Roadhog.

No. 1. *Dress Good.* You have noticed that old Johnny and me wear black suits and so does Sunny James. Besides they dont show dirt as bad.

No. 2. *Sing Good Songs.* People dont like songs they cant dance too. Our most best song is Mama Dont Alow No Giitar Pickin in here. On this won Wichita plays 2 instrumants. He starts out on the electric, lays her down and then plays the flattop. This always ceases to stop the show. Red and Wesley likes the ballards but people aint all that crazy about slow songs. And then Ed Jim Brown is a slow singer.

No. 3. *Keep Yourself Up and Be Clean.* No body can play and sing country music with long hair. Waylen Jenkins has got long hair and you cant hear all of his words sometimes and his band is beatnicks and rock and roll. Kris Krisjefferson has longer hair and you cant hear any of his words at all. Eddie Arnull aint got long hair.

No. 4. *Be Funny.* Everybody likes a good joke. Hears a good joke you can use. There was a chicken when you waved a red flag at her she layed a red egg. When you waved a white flag at her she layed a white egg. When you waved a blue flag at her she layed a blue egg. But Wichita ruint her. He waved a United Staes Americun flag at her and she stripped her gears. Git it?

No. 5. *Be Showmanship.* Always take your hat off when you bow!

No. 6. *Be Courteous.* Dont never tune when somebody else is singing. Dont never blow your nose on stage or in front of a woman. Dont drink and smoke to much in front of your fans. Always pay your band right after the dance. Dont rift in the micaphone.

No. 7. *Play Country Music Instrumants.* Pianos and drums and bugles aint country music instrumants. Pianos is alright in

church but Charlie Ritts, the white Fox if he wants to sit down ought to be playing a steel guitar. He is so fisticated sometimes he sounds like rock and roll and I wished Johnny Cash hadn't have used bugles on Ball of Fire.

No. 8. *Dont Get the Big Head.* The Stafford Brothers have got the big head. After they got me started now they wont give me there home phone numers. I got the home phone numers of some country music stars. They aint got the big head and I dont think they would mind if I gave out there numers. Just to show you hears some I got,

  Bill Andrews—zip code 615 788-1792
  Conroy Titty—zip code 405 647-3069
  Glen Camel—zip code 223-766-3851
  Tom T. Hill—zip code 615 947-0909—If
    you dont find him here call Tooties
    Orchard Longe 478-1846

  Mel Tillus—zip code 615-784-3896—If
    you dont find him either call Tooties
    Orchard Longe again.
  Roger Miller—I aint got his home numer
    but I guess you can find him at King
    on the Road Hotel in Nashville
    Tennessee, Music City USA, Home of
    the Grand Ole Opra

My phone numer is 728-4739 if you want Lester Roahog Moran and his Cadillac Cowboys for your dance, civic affairs, or country music shows you kin call me. Dont call me during the day on the thrid week of each month cause I work swingshift down at the plant and thats my week to work grave yard.

              yourTruely
              Lester Moran
              The Ole Roadhog

⸻⸻⸻⸻⸻⸻⸻⸻⸻⸻⸻⸻⸻⸻

Lester Roadhog Moran with his
Cadillac Cowboys—Wesley, Red, and Wichita.

*Most country stars buy fancy cars.
Hank Williams died in this one.
That's his only son, Hank, Jr., on
the fender. Right: My uncle
Benton Carter, every inch
the country star.*

ARE YOU A COUNTRY STAR?

There's a whole lot more to becoming a country music star than having a voice and a guitar. You will go farther faster if you are also able to think and act like a country star. In the following multiple-choice test, pick the answer or answers (there is more than one correct answer for several questions) that best reflect not what you might believe, but what a real country star believes.

1. Your first record earns you $30,000. As soon as you get the money, you:
A. Pay taxes
B. Buy a new car
C. Put your kids in private school
D. Hire an accountant.

2. You are a famous girl singer who finds out that your husband is sleeping with other women while you are on the road. You:
A. Seek marriage counseling
B. File for divorce
C. Say nothing
D. Find the other woman and warn her off—physically, if necessary.

3. You have a "man to man" agreement with your manager, sealed only by a handshake. Your manager absconds to the Bahamas with your money. You:
A. Call the police
B. Hire a lawyer to sue
C. Decide that the manager, having given his word as a man, is not a man
D. Decide that the manager is a cheat.

4. You are a successful country music entertainer who has just realized that your drug or drinking problem has progressed to the point where you can no longer work. You:

A. Call your doctor

B. Stop the habit and become a Born Again Christian

C. Keep drinking and/or doing drugs

D. Stop your habit, but say nothing about it.

5. You are now such a successful performer that you must start investing your money. You:

A. Get into the bond market

B. Buy gold and diamonds

C. Build a museum dedicated to yourself

D. Open a restaurant named after yourself.

6. Suddenly, you're famous. Just as suddenly, relatives you never knew you had begin coming to "visit." Unfortunately, they seem so happy with you that they forget about going home. You:

A. Let them stay indefinitely

B. Kick them out

C. Have your manager kick them out

D. Give them all jobs in your new business.

7. You've just bought a house and need to furnish it. You:

A. Hire an interior decorator

B. Go to Sears

C. Buy an antique furniture store.

8. You are the world's first Polish country singer. You know that your national origin will attract attention. You:

A. Change your name and hide your ethnic origin

B. Capitalize on your origin by calling yourself "the Singing Pole"

C. Stand up for the dignity of your people.

Loretta Lynn in Hurricane Mills, Tennessee, which she owns.

PEPSI

HURRICANE MILLS
STORE
Bobby & Gould Woods

PEPSI

DEKALB
DEALER

AMERICAN

THIS SALE

GALLONS

AMOCO

AMERICAN

THIS SALE

GALLONS

AMERICAN
REGULAR

9. You are a famous girl singer alone on the road with your band. You see a man in the audience with whom you'd like to spend the evening after the show. You:

A. Go to his place after the show

B. Forget about it and call your husband after the show

C. Have your bus driver sneak the man out of the crowd and into your room

D. Take a cold shower.

10. While you're away on tour, your fifteen-year-old daughter runs away to get married. When you hear the news, you:

A. Send her a wedding present

B. Have your lawyer try to get the marriage annulled

C. Insist that the young couple come and live with you

D. Tell your daughter never to darken your door again.

11. You have just had a fight with your husband and he's given you a black eye. You have a show to do that night. You:

A. Cancel the show

B. Have your husband arrested

C. Wear makeup and do the show anyway

D. Don't wear makeup and tell the audience what happened.

12. A reporter for *Rolling Stone* magazine discovers and prints a story that reveals that the life story you made up for your official biography is untrue. You have to decide how to react. You:

A. Admit everything to Johnny Carson on *The Tonight Show*

B. Send an anonymous death threat to the reporter

C. Include a segment in your show in which you tell the audience about the lies that have been printed about you

D. Say nothing and hope your fans won't hear about it.

Freddy Fender singing at the Austin, Texas, jail. When he became famous, he found that his family had suddenly grown.

Is she not woman enough to take your man? Prove it!

ANSWERS

1. **B.** This should be obvious. Alternatives A, C, and D might be more practical, but none of these things is going to help your public image. Remember, this is your first record, and you want everybody to know you're rich. So you buy a big car. As Waylon Jennings said to Kinky Friedman, when he picked him up walking along a Nashville sidewalk, "Never walk, Hoss. It's bad for your image."

2. **D.** Again, obvious. Everyone knows that women are responsible for seducing lonely married men, who can't help themselves. So you find the woman who slept with your husband and put the fear of God into her. See "Fist City" and "You Ain't Woman Enough (To Take My Man)" by Loretta Lynn.

3. **C.** Men have a code of honor. Signed contracts violate that code because they imply that anyone who wants a signed paper from you is a crook in the first place. If the man with whom you've made an agreement runs out on you, he's violated the code. So he isn't a cheat, or a crook, or anything else. He's something much worse: namely, Not A Man. That's a punishment worse than death.

4. **B or C.** Your choice here depends on what effect you wish to achieve. If you kick the habit and become Born Again, your fans will love you all the more, because country fans just love to forgive famous sinners. Johnny Cash and Merle Haggard took this course, and look how popular they are now. On the other hand, continuing the habit will probably mean that you'll die a tragic death, thus ensuring your place in country music history. People will love your music all the more because everyone will say that you'd have been great had you only lived. See the case of Hank Williams. Choice D is ridiculous, because it won't get you anywhere and nobody will believe you've really stopped your habit anyway.

5. **C or D.** Choices A and B are unthinkable, because buying bonds, gold, or diamonds means you'll have to deal with somebody from New York. You cannot trust those people. Having a museum or a restaurant is not only good publicity—it will make your fans feel closer to you—but you can also hire your relatives to work in these businesses, thus keeping the profits in the family.

6. **C or D.** This happened to Freddy Fender shortly after his recording of "Before the Next Teardrop Falls" became a hit. Reportedly, Freddy's new-found relatives were lodged wall-to-wall in his house. In his case, Huey Meaux, Freddy's manager, sent the "relatives" packing. One of them siphoned the gas from Freddy's pickup before he left. On the other hand, you can make the best of a bad situation by hiring these people to work for you. Relatives will work for much lower pay than regular hired help, so you may save money in the long run.

7. **B or C.** We are assuming that you live in Nashville, which is only now beginning to attract interior decorators. Since you've spent most of your life in motels, and since Sears seems to stock the most motel-like furniture, you're sure to find something you like there. Besides, they deliver. Willie Nelson once bought an entire floor of furniture from Sears for a price of $28,000. If you want to be different, buy out the antique store. Everyone will think you have good taste. Better yet, convert your home into an antique

store. Johnny and June sell stuff from their house at their museum in Hendersonville.

8. **A or B.** Choice C, while it may be a moral thing to do, will ensure your failure as a star. Country fans are made uneasy by the foreign or the unknown. Suddenly launching a crusade upholding the dignity of strangers will pass right over their heads. So, you must either change your name or claim to come from Texas (which is possible, since many people of Eastern European origin come from there), or milk your identity—in a humorous manner, mind you—for all it's worth. This will probably mean that you'll have to tell Polack jokes on the Johnny Carson show, but after all, doesn't Dolly Parton tell boob jokes? Doesn't Ronnie Milsap have several record company biographies that begin, "Blind since birth, Ronnie Milsap . . ."? Study the career of Kinky Friedman and the Texas Jewboys.

9. **C.** If you are a girl singer who travels, it's very important to be in cahoots with your bus driver, who probably acts as your road manager and bodyguard as well. The skilled bus driver should be able to pull a man out of a crowd unobtrusively and sneak him in and out of your room with no one the wiser.

10. **C.** This happens more often than you think, so you shouldn't be shocked. After all, you were probably married as a teenager yourself. On the other hand, you know how hard it is for a young couple to survive on their own, so you insist that they live with you, at least until they are 17 and old enough to get a driver's license.

11. **C or D.** Makeup can do wonders for the battered girl singer. If the eye hurts, take a couple of aspirin before going on. Of course if the audience knows who your husband is, you can get a lot of mileage out

of telling the whole story in public. This will make the audience feel sorry for you, and they'll buy your records for the rest of their lives.

12. **C or D.** Never admit anything. If your fans hear of this story, merely deny it, and attack the press from the stage. Everybody knows that journalists are unsympathetic creeps anyhow. If nobody happens to see the story, don't call attention to it. It will probably blow over in no time. See the cases of Hank Williams and David Allan Coe.

Scoring: Give yourself 10 points for each correct answer.
170–190: You are already a country star. Only amateurs are supposed to be taking this test.
120–170: You like country music so much that you moved to Nashville and got a job as a waitress or a mechanic on the chance that a famous star might drop by while you're working.
90–120: You've heard of Johnny Cash and Dolly Parton. You think Hank Williams is still alive.
Below 90: You are from New York.

The battered girl singer: Tammy Wynette after her kidnapping in 1978.

DID YOU HEAR?

The insular world of country music thrives on rumors. Seldom does a day go by in Music City that at least one completely outrageous story isn't circulating through the telephone lines. On the other hand, country musicians do some pretty outrageous things. Below is a sampling of such stories, all of which have been circulated as rumors at one time or another. Some, however, are true. Your job is to figure out which is false and which is true.

1. There is a plan in existence in Montgomery, Alabama, which calls for the body of Hank Williams to be dug up and re-entombed in the toe of a giant cowboy boot. A restaurant would be located in the top of the boot, where diners could view the skyline of Montgomery while enjoying their dinners.

2. Country singer David Allan Coe, "the Mysterious Rhinestone Cowboy," is an ex-convict. At one time Coe served time on Death Row for murdering another convict by battering him to death with the wringer of a mop bucket.

3. John Ritter, star of the television series *Three's Company,* is the son of the late Tex Ritter. Although Tex was mostly famous for his long career in country music, he actually held a law degree from Northwestern University in Chicago.

4. Johnny Cash, a 1980 inductee into the Country Music Hall of Fame, knows what he's talking about when he sings "Folsom Prison Blues," because he's an ex-convict.

5. Dolly Parton's "husband," Carl Dean, is not really her husband. In truth, Dean is the caretaker for Dolly's Nashville farm, and Dolly herself is not married at all.

6. Loretta Lynn, "the Coal Miner's Daughter," is a psychic who can both know the past and read the future simply by looking at your palm.

7. A. P. Carter, the founder of the Carter Family and a member of the Country Music Hall of Fame, was a notorious song appropriator.

Loretta Lynn and Dolly Parton—two of the most gossiped-about women in the business.

8. Tammy Wynette, who loves hospitals just about as much as she loves to sing, plans to enter a Nashville hospital soon in order to have her natural fingernails replaced with facsimiles made of real gold.

9. Patsy Cline, the famous girl singer who died in a plane crash with Randy Hughes, Hawkshaw Hawkins, and Cowboy Copas on March 5, 1963, facilitated her rise to stardom by being notoriously free with her sexual favors.

10. Hank Williams died of a heart attack.

11. Like his ex-roommate Johnny Cash, Waylon Jennings has served time in the penitentiary.

12. Once when his wife, Tammy Wynette, hid the keys to all of their cars, George Jones drove a riding lawnmower ten miles into Nashville just to get himself a bottle of whiskey.

13. Though both duet partners Loretta Lynn and Conway Twitty are married, they share in a long-standing love affair.

14. The late country singer Red Foley, whose recording of "Peace in the Valley" was both a country and pop hit in the fifties, once nearly died from a drug overdose.

15. Willie Nelson's second wife, Shirley, angered that her husband had come home drunk, decided to leave him. Before doing so, she sewed Willie up in the bedsheets and beat him with a broom.

16. Jack Ruby, the man who shot Lee Harvey Oswald on national television, booked Hank Williams in Texas.

17. Dolly Parton's bustline was not always as ample as it now seems. When she began singing in the early sixties, Fred Foster, owner of the Monument label for which she recorded, paid a plastic surgeon to make some additions to Dolly's figure.

18. Western swing star Spade Cooley murdered his wife. As he was beating her mother to death, he told his daughter, "You're going to watch me kill her."

ANSWERS

1. True. Judge Richard Emmett, the executor of Williams' estate, came up with this idea several years ago. Although the boot has never been built, the plan has never been officially tabled.

2. False. Coe is an ex-convict, and he does claim that he killed a fellow inmate with a wringer from a mop bucket because the inmate was making sexual advances toward him. In fact, Coe's earliest publicity flyers were made to look like "wanted" posters and featured the "murder" charge. A check with Marion State Correctional Institute authorities, however, revealed that Coe was never charged with murder—he was never connected with a prison murder at all. Prison officials also deny that Coe ever served time on Death Row, although Coe

disputes this, saying that L-Block, where he was incarcerated, was merely another name for Death Row. At the time he served his sentence (for possession of burglary tools), the death penalty had been ruled unconstitutional by the United States Supreme Court.

3. True. John is the son of Tex (real name: Maurice Woodward Ritter), and Tex did have a law degree. In addition, the famed country singer appeared on Broadway in the play *Green Grow the Lilacs,* and in numerous movies.

4. False. Although many people assume that Johnny Cash is an ex-convict because of his famous jailhouse concerts at Folsom and San Quentin prisons, Cash himself has been in jail only twice, for a total of 48 hours. In 1965, the Man In Black was arrested and jailed in El Paso, Texas, on a charge of illegally importing amphetamines from Mexico. He received a suspended one-

Patsy Cline. Was she a "loose woman"?

year sentence. In 1966 he was arrested, but not jailed, for possession of a small amount of marijuana. In 1967 police in a small Georgia town found him wandering aimlessly in the streets one night, apparently drunk. They threw him in jail to sleep it off. Shortly thereafter Cash decided to stop taking pills, and has been in no trouble since then.

5. False. Many people are under the impression that Dolly Parton is not married because her husband, Carl Dean, almost never comes to her shows and is never seen in public. Although this marriage may be considered "odd" by some, Dolly's really married. She met Dean, an asphalt contractor, at the Wishy Washy Laundromat on the first day she came to Nashville in 1964, and they were married soon after. They have no children.

6. It's up to you, but I happen to be a believer. Loretta read my palm the first time I ever met her. Not only did she tell me things I'd never even told my husband, but several events she predicted have come to pass. I was

so spooked by this experience that I've never let Loretta see my hands since.

7. True. Many songs that A. P. Carter claimed he "wrote" were really old folk or parlor songs. The famous "Wildwood Flower," for example, was actually "I'll Twine 'Mid the Ringlets," a song written in 1860 by Maud Irving and J. P. Webster. Carter's version slightly garbles the words of the original, but it's essentially the same song. A. P. also claimed credit for songs that were apparently written by Maybelle Carter. One that the late Mother Maybelle told me she wrote was "You Are My Flower." A. P. got the credit.

8. False. This is an example of one of country music's wilder fantasies and was told to me in all seriousness by a record company executive. Although Tammy Wynette has been in enough hospitals to write a guidebook called *The Best Hospitals in the United States,* she isn't planning to have her fingernails removed.

9. **False.** This is an often-told story and is believed by many country singers. Although it has no basis in fact, it may have started because Patsy Cline, unlike every girl singer who preceded her, became successful without the help of a husband who was also in the business. Cline was also known to have been brash, outspoken, and independent. In country music circles, these qualities can mean only one of two things: a strong man or a "loose" woman.

10. **False.** Hank, who died in the back seat of his 1952 powder-blue Cadillac on January 1, 1953, while en route to a show in Ohio, most probably died of a combination of drugs and alcohol. Hank's mother, Lillian Skipper Stone, flew to Oak Hill, West Virginia, where Hank's body was, immedi-

Clockwise from far left: _Hank Williams and friends at New York's Stork Club. Will his body end up inside a giant cowboy boot? Is Waylon Jennings an ex-convict? Is Loretta Lynn psychic?_

ately after he was discovered. Hank's body was embalmed after a hasty autopsy, and the samples of his blood, urine, and stomach contents were apparently thrown away. Lillian circulated the heart attack story and saw to it that heart failure was listed as the cause of death on his death certificate. The autopsy report indicates that Hank probably suffocated on his own vomit, a common cause of death among drug addicts.

11. **False.** Although Waylon and Cash were roommates at one time, Waylon has never served time in jail. Many fans think that he has because of his tough image and his identification as an "outlaw."

12. Tammy Wynette has often told this story, although once she said the incident occurred in Florida, rather than in Tennessee. However, according to her autobiography, *Stand By Your Man,* and several witnesses, Nashville was the town George Jones headed for on his lawnmower.

13. **False.** Another widely believed rumor that is untrue. Loretta and Conway are a successful duet act, and they often tour together—on separate buses—but they have never had a love affair.

14. **True.** Although Red Foley was perceived as an upright, God-fearing gospel and ballad singer, he was rushed to the hospital to be treated for an overdose of sedatives shortly before he was found dead in an Indiana hotel room in 1968. Foley also drank, was married three times, and had famous public battles with his second wife, Eva Overstreet.

15. **True.** According to Willie, this incident, followed shortly thereafter by a fire that destroyed everything he had in Nashville, was one of the things which made him leave Nashville and become a hog farmer in Texas. Although he failed at hog farming, he did launch a new career from Texas and helped start the country music outlaw movement.

16. **True.** Ruby owned a nightclub in Dallas, and he booked Hank Williams into his club as well as several others in the state.

17. **False.** I suspect the rumor is the result of wishful thinking around Nashville. In fact, Dolly Parton has been rather generously endowed since her high school days.

18. **True.**

THE PERFECT COUNTRY SONG

A few years ago, songwriter Steve Goodman had the idea of trying to write a song that would combine all of the themes of various country songs into one perfect entity. The writer would have to get a train into the song, of course, since the very first million-selling country song was "The Wreck of the Old 97." Jail would have to be mentioned too, because the flip side of "The Wreck of the Old 97" happened to have been "The Prisoner's Song." The song should also say something about Mama, and about drinking, and about rain.

This is what Goodman came up with:

I was drunk the day my mama got out of
* prison,*
And I went to pick her up in the rain,
But before I could get her in my pickup truck,
She got run over by the damned ole train.

Goodman did pretty well, except that there's no mention of cheatin' in his song, nor of the all-important cowboy, nor of religion. There is a death in the song, so it could count as a sad song, but somehow it doesn't really *seem* sad. Still, no one else has come up with a better version, so Steve holds the honor of having written the world's only almost-perfect country song.

Historically, country songs have been a reliable barometer of social changes in Middle America, in part because one of the earliest forms of what would become country songs were written about actual events. Called broadsides, or saga songs, the tunes were oral newspapers, telling the stories of happenings close by or far away. The wreck of the ship *Titanic* is an example of how an event inspired one such song, which has survived to this day. In the late forties a popular country song told of the death of little Kathy Fiscus, a 6-year-old child who fell down a dry well pipe near her home in San Marino, California, and died. In our own day few such songs are heard, and only one songwriter, the venerable Red River Dave McEnery, still makes a living by writing them (see page 105).

A cousin of the saga song is the tribute song, a country staple that thrives today. The tribute song is written about some famous

character after his or her death. There are tributes written to Jimmie Rodgers, Hank Williams, Amelia Earhart, and Jim Reeves, and recently we witnessed a spate of them after the respective deaths of Elvis Presley and John Lennon. Such songs can be profitable for the songwriter and recording artist who do them. Shelby Singleton, owner of Sun Records in Nashville, once ruefully related to me that he could have made a million dollars with a song called "The Battle Hymn of Lt. Calley," a song about the soldier involved in the massacre at My Lai in Vietnam, "if only Nixon hadn't pardoned him."

The modern country song, while often based on real events, is both more personal and more abstract than the story song or the tribute song, because the modern song usually deals with emotions and thoughts rather than events. People who've written "cheatin' songs," for example, often explain that the impetus for writing the song came from personal experience. Drinkin' songs are frequently generated in the same way, as are the many sad songs that inhabit the country music popularity charts.

A fourth class of country song is the one based on some kind of ideal or hero. In country music's early days, this hero was often depicted as a wanderer who was sometimes down and out. Both Jimmie Rodgers and the Carter Family had such characters in their songs. Just after 1930, when the "singing cowboy" fad was popular with moviegoers, the country music hero adopted a similar style, even wearing western dress. This prototype lasted until the dramatic end of Hank Williams' meteoric career in 1953, after which country music singers began to imitate

Hank's "tormented genius" role—a man successful in music but a failure at life.

The Hank role was refined in the 1970s by the "outlaw" branch of country music, when the cowboy was again adopted as a hero. This time, however, the cowboy was more antihero, a man (almost no women used this pose) who had integrity and strength and confidence enough to buck the waves of convention. Thus, both Willie Nelson and Waylon Jennings dared to grow shoulder-length hair and criticize the Nashville music business establishment—all on their own, if necessary. This cowboy valued freedom above all things, and if freedom's demands made one lonely and unhappy, so be it. Typically, country music song lyrics changed as the heroes did: "Cool Water" was replaced by "Honky Tonk Heroes" and "Mamas, Don't Let Your Babies Grow Up to Be Cowboys."

Right now, country songs about heroes seem to be in a transitional phase, perhaps because there is a shortage of bona fide heroes to imitate. The outlaws are getting old and commonplace; there hasn't been a real revolution in the country music field for about ten years. Consequently the songs seem to use the same tried and true formulas over and over. We've still got cheatin', drinkin', class solidarity (as in the song "I Was Country When Country Wasn't Cool"), love, and nostalgia. If history does repeat itself, a new hero will come along pretty soon and add one more element to those required for the perfect country song.

Meanwhile, I'll tell you what near-perfect songs to remember.

Loretta Lynn listens to demonstration tapes. Will she find the perfect country song?

THE TEN BEST CHEATIN' SONGS

"Your Cheatin' Heart" by Hank Williams
"Almost Persuaded" by Billy Sherrill and Glenn Sutton
"Slippin' Around" by Floyd Tillman
"You Ain't Woman Enough (To Take My Man)" by Loretta Lynn
"Window Up Above" by George Jones
"Don't Let Me Cross Over" by Carl and Pearl Butler
"Please Help Me, I'm Falling (In Love With You)" by Hal Blair
and Don Robertson
"Last Cheater's Waltz" by Sonny Throckmorton
"If You Loved a Liar (You'd Hug My Neck)" by E. Montgomery
and George Jones
"One Has My Name, the Other Has My Heart" by Hal Blair,
Eddie Dean, and Dearest Dean

In a way, the so-called "cheatin' song" has been with us since the first man or woman left his or her lover. "Wildwood Flower," for example, is a kind of cheatin' song because it's about a faithless man who had "gone and neglected his frail wildwood flower." These songs, however, usually concerned sweethearts, not married people. Songs about full-blown adultery didn't become widely popular until the forties, when men who were soldiers had the opportunity to cheat on their wives, and wives who worked in the wartime factories left their homes and were exposed to the wicked world for the first time. The cheatin' song's development also parallels the development of honky tonk drinking songs. Prior to World War II, the country music audience was largely rural and religious, but during and after the war, and continuing through to the early sixties, rural Southerners left home for jobs in the North, where liquor-by-the-drink was almost universally allowed and where it was relatively simple to "get into trouble." Cheatin' songs, therefore, are a reflection of massive social upheaval.

Still, the country music audience held onto many of the virtues that they had been taught at home, and so the lyrics of the best cheatin' songs document the guilt that goes with the act of falling in love with someone other than one's spouse. Cheatin' is a definite sin for which you'll pay, as Hank Williams notes so eloquently in "Your Cheatin' Heart." "Almost Persuaded" is a quasi-psychological study of a person who is sorely tempted to sin but doesn't; and "Slippin' Around" reminds us that cheating involves the sin of lying as well as adultery. Most cheatin' songs reflect one or more of these aspects, even today. Free love just hasn't caught

Cheatin' songs originated in honky tonks during World War II.

on with the country crowd—at least officially.

Loretta Lynn's "You Ain't Woman Enough" has a unique twist to it, because the woman who is sinned against does not give up and admit powerlessness but instead fights for "what's hers," emphasizing the illegitimacy of a lover's claim on a married person. Sonny Throckmorton's "Last Cheater's Waltz" offers still another perspective on the problem; in his song, the cheater, a woman, is depicted as knowing the futility of her position, but, even so, cannot stay away from the object of her love.

Many cheatin' songs are written from personal experience. Loretta Lynn has always said that "You Ain't Woman Enough" was directed at a specific person. Songwriter Hal Blair, one of the co-writers of "One Has My Name, the Other Has My Heart" told Dorothy Horstman, in an interview for *Sing Your Heart Out, Country Boy,* "This song is a true story and concerned me. . . . I was engaged to a girl when I came home from overseas, and due to a misunderstanding, we were not married. I, very brilliantly, on the rebound, married someone else. The storyline of the song is very simple and self-explanatory." The song, incidentally, is one of the earliest cheatin' songs, and Blair told Horstman that certain church leagues banned it.

Today, many listeners see the old-fashioned cheatin' song as a bit of a joke, and blatantly ridiculous songs, such as "Your Wife's Been Cheatin' on Us Again" are both recorded and listened to. Yet the old songs, with their accounts of genuine moral dilemmas, remain as classics from a time when right and wrong were much simpler to define.

THE TEN BEST SONGS OF CLASS CONSCIOUSNESS

"(We're Not) The Jet Set" by Bobby Braddock

"Okie From Muskogee" by Merle Haggard

"Sold American" by Kinky Friedman

"Coal Miner's Daughter" by Loretta Lynn

"Detroit City" by Mel Tillis and Danny Dill

"Sixteen Tons" by Merle Travis

"The Streets of Baltimore" by Tompall Glaser and Harlan
  Howard

"Fightin' Side of Me" by Merle Haggard

"Take This Job and Shove It" by David Allan Coe

"Rednecks, White Socks, and Blue Ribbon Beer" by Bob McDill,
  Waylon Hollyfield, and Chuck Neese.

Rich people are not supposed to like country music. Neither are foreigners, Catholics, Jews, blacks, or people with college educations. That doesn't mean that these kinds of people *can't* like country music; it just means that the average country song isn't written with these groups in mind as the audience. A country songwriter writes about him- or herself and the experiences of family or friends. If lucky, the songwriter will have had experiences that are similar, if not identical, to those experienced by the so-called "ideal country audience."

Supposedly, the people who comprise the ideal country music audience are not rich; some may even be very poor. They have average educations, regular jobs, are married and have children, are just this side of conservative politically, and are proud to have been able to make enough money to allow their families to live comfortably. A few

A VFW dance in Texas—red necks, white socks, and Blue Ribbon beer. Opposite: Country fans in Kentucky—not the Jet Set.

years ago the members of this audience would have been expected to be from one of the Southern states, but today these (mythical) country fans may come from anywhere. In short, the typical country fan today is envisioned as the "Average American Joe."

In reality, the country fans I've encountered have been as various in kind as raindrops. They are rich, poor, black, white, educated, uneducated, religious, atheistic—and come from anywhere between Grinder's Switch and Timbuktu. Nonetheless, there is some part of all of these people that identifies itself with the "average" country fan, and the social class to which that fan is presumed to belong.

Thus country songs about social classes tend to celebrate this averageness. In

"(We're Not) The Jet Set," as recorded by Jones and Wynette, the protagonists get together in Rome, Paris, and Athens—Georgia, Texas, and Tennessee, respectively. The "Okie From Muskogee" watches the hippies on television and sees nothing but the trappings—the drugs, the flag burnings, the contempt for the law—and celebrates his own rightness and ordinariness and continuity. This same approach applies to the people in "Fightin' Side of Me," which is a bit more mean-spirited than "Okie," and in "Rednecks, White Socks, and Blue Ribbon Beer." Everyone's alike, together, and in sympathy with one another against what is probably a hostile and threatening outside world.

Another kind of class song is the one in which the subject of the song is an outsid-

er, away from home and kindred spirits. In "Detroit City," the singer has let his family think that he's doing fine at his well-paying, but spiritually empty, job on the assembly line. In truth all he wants is to go home, even if he has to hop a freight to do it. A similar situation applies in "Streets of Baltimore." This time a couple has gone to the big city, and the wife has succumbed to the attractions of the neon lights, makeup, and nightlife. Both these songs are a direct result of the South-to-North migrations of the fifties.

In the third kind of class song, the protagonist admits that what he or she must do in life is perhaps unfair, but nevertheless unavoidable. "Sixteen Tons" is a song about a coal miner who works unendurable hours for a pittance, but is still proud of the fact that he's tougher than most men. "Coal Miner's Daughter," the famous Loretta Lynn song, extols the dignity of the coal miner in a similar way and extends that mantle to his family, who must suffer in other ways.

Finally, David Allan Coe's militant "Take This Job and Shove It" is notable for its aggressive stand against those in authority. Historically, the country song of social consciousness always stopped short of blaming anything more specific than "fate" for the condition in which the people in the song found themselves. In this song—something of a first for country music—there is outright defiance of the boss, who's advised in no uncertain terms as to what he can do with his orders and his meager paycheck. The song was enormously popular when it was released in 1977, and it's become a bit of a classic since, especially among labor unionists.

The song of class consciousness should be with us as long as there is a constitutional guarantee of free speech and a country music recording industry, for more than any other, this kind of song seems to unify the diverse groups of country fans in America.

THE BEST TRADITIONAL COWBOY SONGS

"Tumbling Tumbleweeds" by Bob Nolan

"Ghost Riders in the Sky" by Stan Jones

"Cool Water" by Bob Nolan

"Back in the Saddle Again" by Ray Whitley and Gene Autry

"When the Work Is Done Next Fall" by D. J. O'Malley

"Don't Fence Me In" by Cole Porter

"Cattle Call" by Tex Owens

The fact that one of the most famous cowboy songs of all time—"Don't Fence Me In"—was written by Broadway songwriter Cole Porter should give you an idea of what the first wave of cowboy heroes was like. These songs were classified as country music only because they dealt with a supposedly country theme: cowboys worked outdoors and so did farmers; both, therefore, were country. In fact most of these early cowboy songs— and the best of them—were written for Hollywood movies during a time when the singing cowboy was a star. In truth, about the only thing that most country singers had to do with movie cowboys is that both wore the same rather glamorous clothes while they were working. The cowboy garb helped the country singer's public image immensely, because it gave dignity to performers who'd been ridiculed when they'd worn the older country outfits—overalls and bandanas. Country performers stayed with the western style of clothes, at least for stage outfits, much longer than did actors, and so "country" and "western" eventually became synonymous, merely because the performers dressed alike.

The songs of these first country cowboys became national, rather than country, music—classics because they were disseminated by the movies, a much more powerful media outlet than country music would have for years to come. Still, the songs did create a kind of hero that country musicians sought to emulate and incorporate into their value systems. American through and through, the cowboy lived close to nature, and he valued his independence (there were next to no female cowboys at the time, although Patsy Montana did score a million seller with her record of "I Want to Be a Cowboy's Sweetheart" in 1936).

He was always on the right side of the law, and he preferred loneliness to giving up his freedom. This cowboy didn't have a questioning bone in his body; he took life as it came and never complained.

Most of the people who wrote the first cowboy songs weren't real cowboys at all, but men who'd come west to Hollywood seeking work in the movies. Bob Nolan, the writer of the beautiful "Tumbling Tumbleweeds" and "Cool Water," and a founding member of the Sons of the Pioneers, whose close harmonies came to be the hallmark of the singing cowboy, was from Canada. Many of his songs were reportedly written simply because of the sheer wonder he felt at the unfamiliar western landscape. Gene Autry, co-writer of "Back in the Saddle Again," had a rural upbringing in Oklahoma, but he also had worked as a telegraph operator. He eventually came to the "National Barn Dance" as a singing star and had one hit, "That Silver-Haired Daddy of Mine," before successfully auditioning for a singing cowboy spot with Republic Studios, an enterprise that he now owns.

Both D. J. O'Malley and Tex Owens, writers of "When the Work Is Done Next Fall" and "Cattle Call," respectively, had actual experience as real cowboys, and perhaps it is for this reason that their songs were more pessimistic than Nolan's. O'Malley, a cowboy in eastern Montana, wrote the song first as a newspaper poem, about a cowboy whose dying wish is to return home to his mother after his work for the year is finished. Owens, the father of Laura Lee McBride, the first girl singer with Bob Wills and his Texas Playboys, worked as a cowboy on the King Ranch in Texas before becoming a singer. He told Dorothy Horstman that he wrote his song while sitting in the lobby of a radio station. It was snowing outside, Owens said, and he began to remember how he'd fed the cattle in Texas by hand when the weather was bad. Sitting there in that lobby, he began to hear the cattle lowing as they gathered around the feed wagon. He wrote his song, he said, because he felt sorry for those cows.

THE BEST OUTLAW COWBOY SONGS

"Willie the Wandering Gypsy and Me" by Billy Joe Shaver
"Honky Tonk Heroes" by Billy Joe Shaver
"Ride 'Em, Jewboy" by Kinky Friedman
"Ladies Love Outlaws" by Lee Clayton
"Good-Hearted Woman" by Waylon Jennings and Willie Nelson
"Mamas, Don't Let Your Babies Grow Up to Be Cowboys" by Ed
    and Patsy Bruce
"We Are the Cowboys" by Billy Joe Shaver
"Red-Headed Stranger" by Willie Nelson
"The Silver Tongued Devil and Me" by Kris Kristofferson

About 1970, a new kind of cowboy started showing up in Nashville. These weren't the kind of cowboys who wore white hats and saved the homestead from the Indians. As often as not, these cowboys wore black, and while they were always polite to women and children, they allowed one to believe that they'd be dangerous as rattlesnakes if crossed. Writer Dave Hickey named them the Telecaster Cowboys, after the sleek, slim electric guitars they favored. Waylon Jennings, who was a founding member of the group, described himself as a "psychedelic cowboy," in accordance with the then fashionable trend in hallucinogenic drugs. Hazel Smith, who worked with the boys at Tompall Glaser's studio—called "Hillbilly Central" by the in-crowd—gave them their official name when asked by a radio interviewer to characterize these new people in country music. Hazel knew that the cowboy image was apt, but that the term might be confused with the earlier batch of country cowboys. Then she remembered the title of a

Lee Clayton song that Waylon Jennings had recorded, "Ladies Love Outlaws," and thus was the outlaw movement in country music christened.

As the outlaws became more and more popular, members of the movement tired of the label, but in the beginning, when Jennings, Tompall Glaser, Kris Kristofferson, Willie Nelson, and several other pickers and singers were fighting for freedom from the assembly-line-like production techniques of Nashville's business-as-usual record companies, the word "outlaw" suited them perfectly. That they believed deeply in what they were doing is evidenced by the fact that the outlaws wrote and performed some of the best country songs of the decade, songs that expressed a different attitude toward life.

Historically, country songs have been passive, taking the position that while life may be unfair, it can't be changed. The outlaw songs, however, said: "Maybe *your* life can't be changed, buddy, but mine can, and I'm headin' for Mexico." Or wherever.

These cowboys valued freedom over all else—including family, home, and friends. In fact those very ties were often the reason that these cowboys took it on the lam. In "Willie the Wandering Gypsy and Me," a song that Tex Ritter thought brilliant, the singer, whose wife's waiting with an overdue baby, calls up his friend to go out adventuring anyhow. These cowboys, while they certainly appreciated the female sex, weren't exactly domesticated.

Actually, the outlaws were a bit immature by today's standards, and usually, they admitted it in song after song. They were nothing more or less than honky tonk heroes, out to have a little fun without causing too much damage, if possible, and promising nothing to anybody. There's even a certain schizophrenia involved: Kris Kristofferson explains in "The Silver Tongued Devil and Me" that the fellow who does all the bad stuff in his name really isn't him at all, but a soul possessed by a slick-talking, smooth customer from you-know-where.

There's also a kind of conceit that goes with the role. "Ladies Love Outlaws," proclaims Lee Clayton's song, and "Good-Hearted Woman," another song in this vein, explains that the ladies just can't help themselves when it comes to loving an outlaw, charming devil that he is. If you don't like it, then too bad, sing the outlaws, advising the mamas to keep their young boy children away from evil influences like themselves.

After the initial macho posturing had been traded on, some of the outlaws wrote songs that were more analytical than those I've mentioned. Kinky Friedman's "Ride 'Em, Jewboy" applies the metaphor of the alienated cowboy, who's often a social castoff, to the endless wanderings of the Jewish people. Another song that is rather poignant is Billy Joe Shaver's "We Are the Cowboys,"

written late in the decade. Here Shaver, author of "Willie the Wandering Gypsy and Me" and "Honky Tonk Heroes," does an about-face to say that cowboys have a duty to do nothing less than save the world.

Willie Nelson's "Red-Headed Stranger," both as a song and as the concept album, captures this whole cycle, as the protagonist of the song goes from being a half-crazed murderer to a sane and accepting family man.

Today the outlaws have softened their stance. Waylon Jennings, as physically menacing as ever, is a grandfather a couple of times over; Willie Nelson's being hailed as America's new Bing Crosby; Kris Kristofferson is a romantic lead in the movies; and Tompall Glaser has rejoined his brothers in a trio act. But these men created a new kind of hero for country music, and their songs will let this hero live for a long, long time.

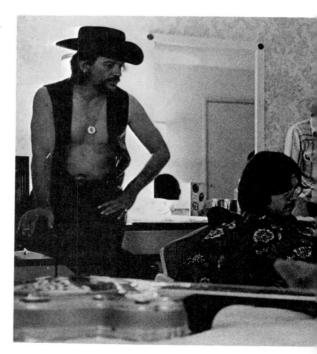

Below: *Mamas, don't let your babies grow up to be cowboys—Waylon Jennings and the Waylors, somewhere on the road.* Right: *Billy Joe Shaver, a cowboy.*

DEAD KIDS AND COUNTRY MUSIC

"Me and Little Andy" by Dolly Parton
"Don't Make Me Go to Bed (And I'll Be Good)" by Hugh Cross
"The Drunken Driver" by Lynn Davis
"Our Baby's Book" by Ernest Tubb
"The Funeral" by Luke the Drifter (Hank Williams)

One reason people ridicule country music is because so many of its songs are maudlin and sentimental. Nowhere is this characteristic so obvious as in the numerous songs written about the deaths of small children—the "dead kid songs," as they're facetiously called. It's true. These songs *are* maudlin, and in a way the lyrics take a cheap shot at the emotions of Americans, who, as a nation, have elevated the child to a godlike status in the home.

On the other hand, there are reasons that these songs are still included in the repertoire of country music. First, this kind of song first became popular in the Victorian era, where sentimentality, along with goriness and tragic deaths, were In things. The songs lasted longer in rural America than in the rest of the country, and were gradually worked into the body of the folk music of the time. One that's still heard now and then is "Put My Little Shoes Away," written in 1873 by Samuel Mitchell and Charles E. Pratt. This one, in which the plucky, but fatally ill, child nobly urges his mother to save his perfectly good new shoes for his younger, healthy sibling, is a good example of the kind of ditty that Victorians seemed to have liked,

combining tragic death with practical household economics. Songs like these really are cruel, but somehow they've hung on.

Other country songs on this subject have a real sense of tragedy to them, because they're about an experience that was all too common in rural America for much too long; an abnormally high infant mortality rate prevailed in areas where there were few doctors, inadequate medical knowledge, and an uneducated population. There are lots of country songs about dead children because a lot of children of country fans died prematurely. In my home county in Kentucky, there's a small cemetery where at least half the graves seem to belong to children. In one instance, there are six square tombstones, all painted silver, ranged in a military row. The graves belong to the children of a single family, and all died a year or two apart in the forties and fifties. Ernest Tubb's "Our Baby's Book" is about the death of his own son, Rodger Dale, who was killed in a car crash while still a baby. Many fans knew exactly what Tubb was singing about, and, Tubb says, he knows of more than three hundred children who've been named "Rodger Dale" because of his song.

In other songs, the death of the child

seems to be a vehicle to make the adults feel guilty about themselves. In "Don't Make Me Go to Bed (And I'll Be Good)," a song made popular by Roy Acuff, who still cries when he sings it, the innocent little child is making too much noise. His parents make him go to bed early. Inevitably the child falls into a fatal delirium, and as he dies, with his anguished parents looking on, all he can say is, "Don't make me go to bed and I'll be good." After hearing that one, people will think twice about punishing their kids.

A child's grave in Kentucky.

The parents who sent their child to bed probably got a bad rap, but in other songs it's perfectly obvious that the wretches deserve what they get. "A Drunkard's Child" dies—we all know why. A little girl whose mother leaves her home at night while she goes to the honky tonks sings "Mommy, Please Stay Home With Me." It turns out to be her swan song. The absolutely most guilt-inducing song, though, is "The Drunken Driver," sung by Molly O'Day. As the song opens, a little boy and girl, their mother dead, are walking along the side of the highway. Suddenly, around the curve comes a careening car, driven by a drunk man. The children are hit. The man jumps out of the car, looks at the children, and screams, "My God, I've killed my son!" That doesn't happen, of course, until the son has time to urge his daddy to change his ways. This song may be maudlin, but it also sends shivers up the spine—the mark of a really great dead kid song.

For this reason, I've ranked Dolly Parton's "Me and Little Andy" as the best of these songs. Dolly has recorded it only once—on her *New Harvest* album—but the listener doesn't get the real effect of the tune unless it's heard live. The plot is straightforward: little child and dog come to the door on a wintry night; he explains that Mommy's gone, Daddy's drunk. He asks for a place to sleep, gets it, and dies. Parton's rendition of the tune is chilling because she uses both the adult's and the child's voice. The child, in a delirious, fey singsong, tells its sad story in childlike rhyme: "London Bridge is falling down./Daddy's drunk again in town." It's scary, as much for the apparent metamorphosis of the buxom Parton into a little child as for anything else. Although Parton always assures the audience that any little kids in attendance will like the song, I'd never let a child of mine hear it. As for me, I cry every time. Call me sentimental.

"The Funeral" by Luke the Drifter—who was Hank Williams' alter ego—is the best of a third genre of dead kid song, the narrative that tells a complete story—in this case the story of a black child's funeral (although the kid is described as an "Ethiopian"). As usual, Hank did it best. Songs that follow the style are generally stinkers. The best example is the "Teddy Bear" saga, originated in the seventies by Red Sovine. Like Victorian songs before it, this style combines themes—in this case, trucks, CB radios, and dead kids. "Teddy Bear" is the "handle" of a crippled child whose daddy died in a truck accident, leaving him his CB rig and his mother a job as a wait-

ress. Teddy Bear bleats his sad story to truckers who pass within his range, and good-hearted souls that they are, the truckers get together to help the kid out. In a later song, "Teddy Bear's Last Ride," the crippled boy dies (Sovine refused to participate in the little tyke's death). That was followed by a tune called "Teddy Bear's Mom," but the public was justifiably sick of the subject by that time.

For one reason or another, these songs still pop up from time to time, usually in spurts. Maybe there are people out there who need to cry but are ashamed to; if so, listening to one of these songs gives them a good excuse.

THE BEST DRINKIN' SONGS

"Whiskey River" by Willie Nelson
"Drinkin' Thing" by Wayne Carson
"She's Actin' Single (I'm Drinkin' Doubles)" by Wayne Carson
"I Gotta Get Drunk" by Willie Nelson
"Misery and Gin" by Merle Haggard
"What Made Milwaukee Famous (Has Made a Loser Out of Me)"
   by George Jones
"Tonight the Bottle Let Me Down" by Merle Haggard
"I Can't Hold Myself in Line" by Merle Haggard
"Two More Bottles of Wine" by Delbert McClinton

Country music songwriters have been preoccupied with the subject of alcohol ever since the first honky tonks began to spring up by the side of the road. For a while, of course, it was more or less taboo to mention

drink in any form, except as an instrument of the devil. In "The Drunken Driver" by Lynn Davis, the inebriated father runs over his own son and daughter on the highway. In "Wreck on the Highway" liquor is to blame for the

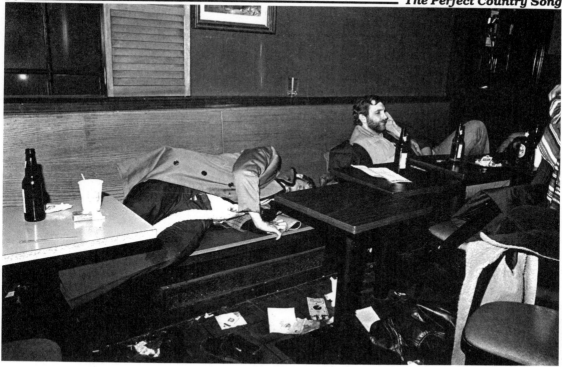

If drinkin' don't kill me . . .

tragedy. Perhaps it was Hank Williams' flagrant alcoholism that made the subject acceptable to the country audience, or perhaps the changing social mores of the fifties made references to drink okay. Whatever the reason, drinking is now written about so often in country tunes that it has become a genre of its own.

But you won't hear a country song express all-out joy for the devil's brew—country songwriters would never write a song like "The Night They Invented Champagne." In country songs the singer doesn't have a drink; he (and it's usually "he") gets drunk—flat-out, heel-walking drunk. Nor is there such a thing as a social drinker in a country song. More often than not, drinking is a lonely occupation, pursued because it kills the pain of living or because the singer has lost all

willpower. Drinking can even become a kind of obligation, as Willie Nelson explains in the slightly humorous "I Gotta Get Drunk."

Nelson's "Whiskey River" expresses the usual attitude, however, as the singer pleads with the "Whiskey River" to take his mind away from the memory of his lost love. Wayne Carson's "Drinkin' Thing" explains, "I got this drinkin' thing to keep from thinkin' thing." Merle Haggard's "I Can't Hold Myself in Line" explains that the lure of drinking has overwhelmed everything else in his world, including his family.

The usual impetus for these binges comes from a broken love affair or an adulterous spouse, as in Carson's "She's Actin' Single (I'm Drinkin' Doubles)"; in Haggard's "Misery and Gin," a man and a woman, both deserted by their respective lovers, share same.

George Jones has created a small subcategory with songs like "What Made Milwaukee Famous (Has Made a Loser Out of Me)," in which the singer is so besotted that he can no longer function at all. Jones seems to have a million of these tunes, with names like "Stand on My Own Two Knees," "Wean Me," and "I've Aged Twenty Years in Five." He might as well be recording for the Alcoholics Anonymous label.

Finally, Delbert McClinton's "Two More Bottles of Wine" is interesting for two reasons. First, the drug of choice here is not whiskey or beer but wine, which until very recently was never served in a country song. Second, the drink in question is being drunk to make life's problems disappear only for the night, not forever. In most country songs, and especially those by George Jones, the drinking is near suicidal—one often gets the impression that the man in the song is really trying to do away with his problems permanently. In McClinton's song there is at least some hope that the guy will live to have tomorrow's hangover. This is encouraging; perhaps it's a sign that country music is beginning to handle its lifelong problem.

George Jones knows whereof he sings.

THE BEST GOSPEL SONGS

"I'll Fly Away" by Albert E. Brumley
"Keep on the Sunny Side of Life" by A. Blenkenhorn and J. H. Entwisle
"Will the Circle Be Unbroken?" by A. P. Carter
"The Great Speckled Bird" by Rev. Guy Smith
"I Saw the Light" by Hank Williams
"Gospel Ship" traditional
"When God Comes to Gather His Jewels" by Hank Williams
"Amazing Grace" traditional
"The Tramp on the Street" by Grady and Hazel Cole
"Precious Memories" by J. B. F. Wright

Some scholars feel that the gospel, or religious, song is the basic source of all country music. It's certain that the gospel style of singing—emotional and intense—is the inspiration for the singing styles of every great country artist, from Roy Acuff to Hank Williams to George Jones to Kitty Wells, and moreover, the teachings of Christian fundamentalism that inform the gospel song, are also part of the fabric of both country music and the lives of its musicians. Even today, it is not unusual to find allusions to God, religion, or morality in a commercial country song, and there isn't a country singer around who doesn't at least pay lip service to the "old-time religion."

The fundamentalism that inspired the gospel song is not quite the same as the fundamentalism espoused by modern movements such as the Moral Majority. To the old-time rural Southern fundamentalist, religion was often the only bright spot in an otherwise bleak life. This religion taught people that life is a burden to be borne in exchange for the rewards of the hereafter, and therefore, there's no use complaining about one's lot in life, because whatever happens is God's will. This is the source of the passive attitudes one finds in many country songs: someone may lament his lot, but he can't change it.

Religious teachings also account for the schizophrenic attitudes of many country singers, especially males. The church teaches that the entertainment business and all its accoutrements are vanities and the work of the devil, and therefore the country singer is doomed from the start by virtue of his occupation. This is an uncomfortable position to be in, especially if you believe that the devil and hell are real, physical things. Perhaps Jerry Lee Lewis, who once attended Waxahatchie Bible College in Texas, best exemplifies this kind of conflict. Almost anyone who knew Lewis in his wilder days will tell you that it wasn't unusual to see Jerry Lee holding a Bible in one hand and a bottle of whiskey in the other. Hank Williams went so far as to create an alter ego named Luke the Drifter to record religious songs.

So, the gospel song, if not the root of country music, is at least the medium from which it sprang. Gospel songs are the most emotional of the country songs, and a good one can make the listener simultaneously happy and sad. The happy songs, like "I'll Fly Away," "Keep on the Sunny Side," and "Gospel Ship," all preach the joys of the glorious afterlife. The sad ones, like "The Tramp on the Street," "Precious Memories," and "Will the Circle Be Unbroken?," all have some element of nostalgia for past events as the basis of their sadness. The latter emotion is carried over into many country songs, where loss—be it of a lover, a parent, or a home—is the basis of the plaint.

Finally, there are a few gospel songs that are nearly surreal in their imagery. The Rev. Guy Smith's "Great Speckled Bird" is one such song. Based on a verse from Jeremiah—"Mine heritage is unto me as a speckled bird, the birds round about are against her; come ye assemble all the beasts of the field, come to devour"—it depicts the true church as the bird, and other churches, which ridicule the true church, as hostile birds. In the singing, however, it's possible for the listener to imagine God as the speckled bird, perhaps a brilliant bird of paradise, surrounded by flames, hovering before one's eyes.

Unfortunately, modern gospel music, like country music, tends to consist of watered-down versions of the powerful themes of salvation and divine retribution. Often the songs are little more than "Have-A-Nice-Day-With-Jesus" affairs. Only bluegrass musicians still sing with a little of the old fire.

THE BEST PRISON SONGS

"In the Jailhouse Now, #2" by Jimmie Rodgers
"Folsom Prison Blues" by Johnny Cash
"I'm Here to Get My Baby Out of Jail" by Karl Davis and Harty Taylor
"The Prisoner's Song" by Guy Massey
"(I'm a Lonesome) Fugitive" by Liz and Casey Anderson

Prison songs have been a part of country music since its beginning. "The Prisoner's Song," with its familiar line "If I had the wings of an angel, o'er these prison walls I would fly," sold a million copies in 1924. Johnny Cash, "the Man in Black," is identified with prisons and prisoners not because he is an ex-convict (he isn't), but because of his million-selling album *Live at Folsom Prison*, with its lead song, "Folsom Prison Blues." Merle Haggard, who had a hit with Liz and Casey Anderson's "Fugitive," actually is an ex-convict. When Johnny Cash made his

Johnny Cash wrote "Folsom Prison Blues" in the fifties.

Live at San Quentin album, Merle was in the audience of inmates.

The appeal of prison songs to country audiences probably lies in the fact that prisoners are helpless. Many country music lovers, tied to a job on an assembly line or a farm where the weather dictates their fortunes, feel much the same. Then, of course, there are not a few people who either have been imprisoned or who know someone who has. This probably accounts for the appeal of a sentimental song like "I'm Here to Get My Baby Out of Jail," a story song about an aged mother who offers to work out bail for her son, only to die in his arms when he is freed.

Besides the fact that prison is a familiar metaphor to country audiences, it must also be remembered that the audience is not necessarily unsympathetic toward prisoners, who, after all, may be victims of the same power structure that oppresses the lower economic classes at large. The outlaw Jesse James, for example, was said to have been a hero to many country people because of his unfailing kindness toward them. There is also a romantic side to prisoners, and it's this romance that makes the image of the outlaw so attractive.

While many songs have been composed about prison and prisoners, few have been particularly well written. Jimmie Rodgers' "In the Jailhouse Now, #2" is the best because it stands so well as a *song*, as opposed to a social document. Its tunefulness, humor, and wry good nature are the hallmarks of a Jimmie Rodgers song, and it's impossible to hear it played by someone else without thinking of the old Singing Brakeman.

THE SADDEST COUNTRY SONGS

"I'm So Lonesome I Could Cry" by Hank Williams
"It's Not Supposed to Be That Way" by Willie Nelson
"Old Shep" by Red Foley and Willis Arthur
"The Grand Tour" by Norro Wilson, Chip Taylor, and George Richey
"Born to Lose" by Ted Daffan
"Cold, Cold Heart" by Hank Williams
"There Goes My Everything" by Dallas Frazier
"Misery and Gin" by Merle Haggard
"Oh, Lonesome Me" by Don Gibson

Country music is often ridiculed because so many of its songs seem to be self-pitying and maudlin. The fact of the matter is that many are. If you really want to get depressed, it can be done almost instantly by listening to the songs listed above and drinking a bottle of whiskey all by yourself. The singers in these songs are *miserable,* and not quietly miserable either. These guys are going up the walls they're so miserable.

The fact that all of these songs were written by men is no coincidence. While Northern men are not supposed to show emotion, Southern men are allowed to express their feelings in public in two places: in church and in a country song. Most of these sad songs concern the breakup of a love affair or marriage, a universal experience if ever there was one. One, Red Foley's and Willis Arthur's "Old Shep," is about a boy who has to shoot his faithful dog companion when the dog gets old and ill. It sounds silly, but if you've had a couple of beers, "Old Shep" can make you cry.

However, there is more than trite emotion and self-pity in the best of these songs. In Hank Williams' "I'm So Lonesome I Could Cry," the pain is existential, with its image of "the silence of a falling star" and the question "did you ever hear a robin weep?" Similarly, in Willie Nelson's "It's Not Supposed to Be That Way" (reportedly written for his drummer, Paul English, after English's wife's suicide), the pain of loss is almost palpable, the lover's absence piercing.

In other songs the feeling of sadness is dependent on the singer's ability to convey it. George Jones's rendition of "The Grand Tour," a song in which the singer takes a friend on a tour of his house after his wife has left him, wouldn't be nearly so effective without Jones's mournful, wailing voice. Ironically, George Richey, one of the co-writers of "The Grand Tour," married Tammy Wynette, Jones's ex-wife and still his true love. Like Jones's song, Ted Daffan's "Born to Lose" came to life for millions of people only after R&B singer Ray Charles cut it for his

country album in the early sixties. No one has ever made "Cold, Cold Heart" sound as sad as Hank Williams himself did, even though the song was cut by Tony Bennett, who had a national hit with it. Merle Haggard's mournful "Misery and Gin" also seems tailor-made for his voice alone.

Whether the sadness of a song rests with the words themselves or the ability of the singer to convey emotion, there is no question that songs of this nature will continue to flourish in the country music field, where having a good, long, drunken cry is as refreshing to the fans as a good long session with a psychotherapist. Besides, who needs a shrink when we've got George Jones and Merle Haggard?

RED RIVER DAVE AND "THE BALLAD OF PATTY HEARST"

Variously billed as the "World's First Television Star," the "Last of the Yodeling Cowboys," and, for a time, the "Singing, Yodeling Cowboy Preacher," Red River Dave McEnery is one of country music's most lovable eccentrics and its most prolific writer of the "saga" or story song based on current events—he once wrote 52 such songs in a twelve-hour period while chained to a piano in San Antonio, Texas. "Amelia Earhart's Last Flight" is Red River Dave's most famous song, the one he sang on television from the RCA Pavilion at the 1939 World's Fair (accounting for his "World's First Television Star" billing). Recently, Dave has written "The Ballad of Three-Mile Island," "Reverend Jimmy Jones," and "When Ol' Bing Crosby Said Goodbye."

*Opposite: **Nobody could sing a sad song like ole Hank.** **Right:** **Red River Dave, author of "The Ballad of Patty Hearst" and thousands of other tribute and saga songs.***

It's Red River Dave's flair for publicity that sets him apart from the pack, however. In addition to his songwriting marathon in San Antonio, Dave has also operated a "church for country musicians" from a room in the Hall of Fame Motel in Nashville, where he did rope tricks while preaching and where he delivered the world's first sermon written entirely in CB language. (Sample: "You say you like beavers [girls]? Well, Good Buddy, Jesus had beavers following him. There was Mary Magdalene, Martha, and others. The Big Breaker in the Sky forgives sin.") The coup of Dave's career was the writing and recording of "The Ballad of Patty Hearst" in 1974. Originally the song ended with the fiery shootout in Los Angeles which wiped out most of the members of the soi-disant Symbionese Liberation Army. After Patty Hearst was found, however, Dave added another verse, in which he asked the question, "Was she captured or was she rescued?" To publicize the song, Dave ran advertisements in the *Nashville Banner* and *The Tennessean*, asking the public to respond to his musical question. The final results of the Patty Hearst poll were a real sign of the times: 66 percent of the respondents said that the kidnap victim had been captured; only 34 percent felt she'd been rescued.

Dave immediately issued a press release "From the Heart of Music City, U.S.A." quoting his reaction. "I'm disappointed in the percentages," he said. "I believe this is the first time in history that anyone thinks a kidnap victim has been captured instead of rescued. I honestly expect more sympathy for a girl who has been through the trial she went through with her SLA captors. I won't change a line of my song. 'The Ballad of Patty Hearst' tells it like it is."

Lest we forget, here is the World's Best Saga Song of 1974:

"THE BALLAD OF PATTY HEARST"
by Red River Dave
(Sung to the tune of "The Battle Hymn of the Republic")

In the State of California, in the year of seventy-four,
One of God's beloved daughters heard a knock upon the door.
Violent men with flaming weapons knocked her boyfriend to the floor.
And kidnapped Patty Hearst.
Chorus: Beat your swords now into plowshares
            Beat your swords now into plowshares
            Beat your swords now into plowshares
            Proclaims the Word of God (Isa. 2:4)
Broken-hearted dad and mother prayed to God upon their knees
Then the "Liberation Army" that was known as "Symbionese,"
Made demands of giant ransom ere young Patty they'd release,
Blood money for the poor.
Chorus: Beat your swords now into plowshares
            Beat your swords now into plowshares
            Beat your swords now into plowshares
            O read the Word of God (Jer. 8:21)

Then there came a tape recording and the voice of Patty said,
To her darling dad and mother that she surely would be dead,
If they didn't heed the warning and distribute all that bread,
A ransom for her life.
Chorus: Beat your swords now into plowshares
           Beat your swords now into plowshares
           Beat your swords now into plowshares
           O heed the Word of God (Isa. 61:1)
From the shores of "Blue Hawaii" to the harbors of Cape Cod
God has richly blessed our nation with the harvest of her sod;
Let the "Symbionesian Army" read the blessed Word of God
All children shall be free.
Chorus: Beat your swords now into plowshares
           Beat your swords now into plowshares
           Beat your swords now into plowshares
           Eternal Word of God (Gal. 6:7)
Then there came a bloody shoot-out in the city of L.A.,
God is calling final judgment on the wicked SLA.
Was she victim? Was she willing? Only God will ever know,
Sing her ballad soft and low.
Chorus: Beat your swords now into plowshares
           Beat your swords now into plowshares
           Beat your swords now into plowshares
           O Blessed Word of God (Mat. 7:1)
In the State of California in the year of seventy-five
Government men discovered Patty, there in Frisco still alive.
Was she rescued? Was she captured? Shall we pity her or blame?
Search the scriptures, once again.
Chorus: Beat your swords now into plowshares
           Beat your swords now into plowshares
           Beat your swords now into plowshares
           Read Matthew: seven, one.

THE STRANGEST COUNTRY SONG

The strangest country song in the world—possibly the strangest song ever written—is called "Psycho." It's a song about a mass murderer and was written by blind songwriter Leon Payne, probably during the 1960s and perhaps under the influence of the Alfred Hitchcock film of the same name. One can only suppose what led the man who wrote the country classics "I Love You Because" and "Lost Highway" to also write a song in which a man kills at least four people and one puppy.

Leon Payne was born in Alba, Texas, in 1917, and was educated at the Texas School for the Blind, where he learned to play many instruments, including guitar, piano, organ, trombone, and drums. With a reputation for instrumental virtuosity, Payne joined Bob Wills and his Texas Playboys in 1938, and stayed with the band for several years. After leaving Wills, Payne became peripatetic, hitchhiking across the state of Texas and playing with bands along the road. Meanwhile, according to Landon and Stambler's *Encyclope-*

Elvis Costello, right, *recorded the world's strangest country song, in 1981.*

dia of Folk, Country and Western Music, Payne wrote several thousand songs, and was eventually signed as a contract writer for Hill and Range Music. In the sixties he entered into a ten-year pact with Acuff-Rose, and it was during this period that Payne suffered a serious heart attack and also wrote "Psycho." There is a rumor that he asked that "Psycho" not be recorded until after his death, but that, like other things about Payne, cannot be confirmed.

"Psycho" was probably recorded for the first time by Jack Kittell, for Michael Thevis's GRC label in Atlanta in 1974. The record did not become popular, but one record collector tells me that he heard that a Detroit radio station had played the song, and then kept getting requests for "the song where the guy kills the dog." The Kittell recording went on to become a collector's item, and "Psycho" was forgotten until 1982, when Elvis Costello, the British rock and roll singer with a pronounced fondness for country music, recorded it for the B-side of his British single "Sweet Dreams," on the F-Beat label. "Psycho" now has a whole new audience.

Costello has made a specialty of sounding ominous on record, and his version of "Psycho" is terrifying, especially if one hasn't heard the song before. It's a story song, which begins with the singer talking to his mother, probably over the kitchen table, while she's cooking something for him. In the course of the conversation we learn: 1. that he has killed his ex-girlfriend and her lover; 2. that he almost killed his little brother; 3. that he's unintentionally squeezing his little brother's puppy to death; 4. that he killed a little girl in the park just a while ago; and 5. that he kills his mother as the song ends. Friends, this is a weird song. It beats both "Rubber Room," by Porter Wagoner, and "Daddy, Come and Get Me," by Dolly Parton, as the scariest song in country music.

THE BEST
TRAIN SONGS

"Orange Blossom Special" by Ervin T. Rouse
"Wabash Cannon Ball" by A. P. Carter
"Waiting for a Train" by Jimmie Rodgers
"Train Whistle Blues" by Jimmie Rodgers
"The Wreck of the Old 97" authorship unknown
"I'm Movin' On" by Hank Snow
"The Brakeman's Blues (Yodeling the Blues Away)" by Jimmie Rodgers

---

Just as cars and airplanes are symbols of freedom to today's generation, so trains were to the first country music fans. "The Wreck of the Old 97" was on the flip side of the million-selling "The Prisoner's Song" in 1924, and Jimmie Rodgers, country music's first solo star, known as "the Singing Brakeman" because of his pre–show-business career, wrote and sang several great songs with train themes. Rodgers is to trains as rock star Bruce Springsteen is to cars.

"Orange Blossom Special," of course, is one of country music's most well-known songs; as a fiddle tune, it never fails to bring an audience to its feet. The song was written about a real train of that name, which ran from Miami to New York; it was said to have been "the most powerful train in the world" at one time. The Wabash Cannon Ball was also a real train, which ran between Kansas City and Chicago, but since the authorship of the song is disputed, it's impossible to say whether the song was written about it specifically. "The Wreck of the Old 97" was written about a wreck that occurred on September 27, 1903, as the Southern Railroad's engine was on its way from Washington to Atlanta.

The train as a means of escaping a ruined love affair is the subject of Jimmie Rodgers' "Train Whistle Blues" and Hank

Jimmie Rodgers, "the Singing Brakeman."

Snow's "I'm Movin' On." Trains were also the preferred mode of travel for hobos and men looking for work during the Depression, as Rodgers explains with his "Waiting for a Train."

Train songs died out with the trains themselves, only to be replaced by a new form of transportation—the truck.

THE BEST TRUCK SONGS

"King of the Road" by Roger Miller
"Phantom 309" by Red Sovine
"Six Days on the Road" by Earl Greene and Carl Montgomery
"White Line Fever" by Merle Haggard
"A Tombstone Every Mile" by David Fulkerson
"Convoy" by C. W. McCall

The truck song depends on the popularity of two earlier song genres—the train song and the cowboy song. Like trains, trucks are seen as symbols of freedom; like cowboys, truckers see themselves as modern-day knights errant, traveling alone or in pairs, sharing their nights with each other over the CB radios. The truckers' fondness for this instrument inspired a small craze for CB radio songs, led by C. W. McCall, whose "Convoy" inspired the Sam Peckinpah movie of the same name. In general, however, most truck songs are too "professional" for the average country fan, and so there is a small sub-recording industry that turns out specially made albums of "truckers' favorites." There's even a truck song specialist named Dave Dudley, who's made a modestly successful living by being a truckers' singer.

However, truck songs that capture the general public's attention come around more often than one would imagine, and some, like Roger Miller's "King of the Road" and "Six Days on the Road," are country music standards. "Phantom 309," the story of a ghost trucker who haunts the highways near where his big rig wrecked, is a cult favorite of rock and rollers, and was once recorded by Commander Cody and His Lost Planet Airmen. "White Line Fever" and "A Tombstone Every Mile" were more modest country hits, but still are included on almost every truckers' favorites album.

Oddly enough, there are no country songs about airplanes, nor are pilots known to be particularly fond of country music. Perhaps this is because people who can afford to fly frequently enough to be interested in airplane songs are not included in country music's target audience, or perhaps it's because plane crashes are more terrifying or more infrequent than truck or train accidents. Or maybe airplanes just take us too far from home.

THE TWELVE BEST WOMEN'S SONGS

"It Wasn't God Who Made Honky Tonk Angels" by J. D. Miller
"The Pill" by Lorene Allen
"Coat of Many Colors" by Dolly Parton
"Stand By Your Man" by Billy Sherrill and Tammy Wynette
"Don't Come Home A-Drinkin' (With Lovin' On Your Mind)" by
    Loretta Lynn
"Jolene" by Dolly Parton
"Coal Miner's Daughter" by Loretta Lynn
"Banjo Pickin' Gal" by Lilly May Ledford and John Lair
"You Ain't Woman Enough (To Take My Man)" by Loretta Lynn
"I Don't Care if Tomorrow Never Comes" (recorded by Molly
    O'Day) by Hank Williams
"Seven-Year Ache" by Rosanne Cash
"Harper Valley PTA" by Tom T. Hall

The fact that I've listed only twelve "women's" country songs is an indication of how seldom women country singers are represented. In fact, they're usually called "girl singers," not "women." (One reason for this is that the noun "woman" is considered an insult by some Southerners.) Those women who have succeeded, however, have all been extraordinary, and the lyrics to the songs listed here are more explicit than the lyrics of any popular tune you might think of.

The number-one spot had to go to Kitty Wells's version of Jay Miller's "It Wasn't God Who Made Honky Tonk Angels," simply because it was the first highly popular country song in which the woman singer talked back to a man. In this case, Wells was talking back literally as well as figuratively, since "It Wasn't

God . . ." was written in response to a Hank Thompson hit called "Wild Side of Life."

In that song, which was a hit in 1949, the male singer is astonished to find that God's creations include women who hang around bars, smoke, drink, and who are generally not "wife material." In answer, Wells declares: "It's a shame that all the blame is on us women/It's not true that only you men feel the same/From the start, 'most every heart that's ever broken/Was because there always was a man to blame." Previous to the Wells record, this sentiment was commonly expressed by women, but never made public. Thus, "It Wasn't God . . ." is a milestone.

Were it not for Kitty Wells's historical advantage, Loretta Lynn would win the honors for top country girl singer of all time.

ager, but Loretta herself had more than a little to do with its writing.

Similarly, "You Ain't Woman Enough (To Take My Man)" and "Don't Come Home A-Drinkin' (With Lovin' On Your Mind)" are also outspoken, each in its own way. The former, which is based on a true incident, again finds the woman standing up for her rights—albeit proprietary rights. The latter song is unique, in that it expresses an emotion so universal—to wit, women's impatience with amorous overtures from drunken lovers—that no one ever thought to put it into words before Loretta.

Finally, "Coal Miner's Daughter," Loretta's signature song, evocative and richly detailed, expresses a pride in heritage that is dignified, loving, and dares anyone to make anything of it. Women's groups should study Loretta's lyrics seriously.

"Stand By Your Man," written by Billy Sherrill and Tammy Wynette, and sung by Tammy, is included because it's simply so strong. The song's message—that a woman should hang in a marriage or a love affair no matter what—is perhaps overly rigid. Nonetheless, the song expresses a strongly held belief of the country music female audience: that women are inherently stronger in character than men, and that women are generally responsible for a man's success and/or failure. It's an aspect of the culture that cannot be overlooked.

"Coat of Many Colors," an autobiographical story-song by Dolly Parton, is one of the most beautiful in all country music. The intricate, detailed story of childhood humiliation, with its message—"You're only poor if you choose to be"—echoes another popularly held belief of the audience. Moreover, the little girl who holds her head up in the face of unwarranted humiliation is a character drawn directly from the ranks of the coun-

Loretta's lyrics—in the songs listed here, as well as in numerous others—ought to rank with the writings of Betty Friedan and Simone de Beauvoir for the feminist consciousness they depict. "The Pill," in particular, is notable. The song, while sung in a mildly humorous manner, is deadly serious in its message: that the advent of effective birth control pills for women will liberate them more than any discovery ever made. Several hundred members of Loretta's fan club dropped their membership when this song was released, but Loretta more than made up for it with new fans who were attracted by the song. Incidentally, writing credit for "The Pill" officially belongs to Lorene Allen, Loretta's office man-

Above: Loretta Lynn,
producer Owen Bradley, and
Ernest Tubb. Loretta was
expecting her twins at the
time this picture was taken.
Left: Kitty Wells, "the
Queen of Country Music," at
the Country Music Hall of
Fame and Museum.

try music culture. In this case, of course, it's Dolly herself. "Jolene," another Parton composition, is also included because of the beauty of the song—musically, as well as lyrically. It's a plea from one woman to another—a woman "with shining locks of auburn hair" whose "beauty is beyond compare"—not to take Dolly's man "just because she can." The song ought to become a classic, even though it's extremely difficult to sing.

"Banjo Pickin' Gal," written by John Lair and Lilly May Ledford, is completely unknown in the modern country repertoire, but it may well be the very first country song that described an independent woman. The lyrics of "Banjo Pickin' Gal" are merely an adaptation of an older banjo tune called "Banjo Pickin' Boy." Ledford and Lair adapted it for the Coon Creek Girls, one of the first all-girl groups in the business. Lilly May Ledford believes she wrote and sang the song in the early thirties. Although the tune has innumerable verses, its basic message is that the banjo pickin' gal's gonna go around the world playing her banjo. Her man can come along if he wants, but she isn't going to stay home. Thus it's quite possible that Lilly May Ledford has Kitty Wells beat by twenty years.

Molly O'Day's rendition of Hank Williams' "I Don't Care if Tomorrow Never Comes" is one of the all-time best performances by a woman in country music history. O'Day, whose commercial career lasted only about four years in the late forties, is a better singer than Kitty Wells—I think O'Day is the best fe-

male singer in country music history, period. Nonetheless, because she stayed in the field for such a short time, she is largely unknown, as are her recordings, only one of which is still available in collectors' circles. Her performance of this song has all the emotion and desperation of an Ophelia, thanks to Molly.

"Seven-Year Ache," written and sung by Johnny Cash's daughter Rosanne, is the only modern song to make it on the list. After a brief flurry of activity between 1968 and 1972, girl singers seemed to lapse back into the lovin'/leavin'/cheatin'/cryin' songs. The results were consistently undistinguished. Loretta Lynn stopped writing because of a dispute over the ownership of her publication rights, and Dolly Parton decided to become a pop singer. That left the field open, and Rosanne may fill the gap slightly. In "Seven-Year Ache," the woman ridicules the man who goes to the honky tonk to drown his depression with beer and fast women. The man is shown to be a fool, but it's pretty apparent that the woman believes that condition is temporary, and that he'll show up sooner or later. In short, she refuses to be a victim.

Finally, there is "Harper Valley PTA," a song that is somewhat dated and that perhaps belongs more in the category of social comment. However, its story of small-town hypocrisy does have a strong woman as its central character, a woman who's divorced and who's rearing a daughter. In those respects it's absolutely modern, and one of barely a handful of songs that include such a female character.

THEME SONGS

Just about every country performer has a theme song—either one he or she has written and which has become inseparable from the writer, or one which he or she has made so popular that the song is forever after identified with the singer. Match the singer with the song.

1. "Wabash Cannon Ball"
2. "Blue Moon of Kentucky"
3. "Whiskey River"
4. "Stand By Your Man"
5. "Waltz Across Texas"
6. "Keep on the Sunny Side"
7. "Coal Miner's Daughter"
8. "Folsom Prison Blues"
9. "Coat of Many Colors"
10. "Detroit City"
11. "Your Cheatin' Heart"
12. "The Race Is On"
13. "I've Got a Tiger by the Tail"
14. "Okie From Muskogee"
15. "Harper Valley PTA"
16. "Slippin' Around"
17. "T for Texas"
18. "It Wasn't God Who Made Honky Tonk Angels"
19. "Walkin' After Midnight"
20. "Me and Bobby McGee"
21. "Peace in the Valley"
22. "Luckenbach, Texas"

Bobby Bare
Red Foley
Dolly Parton
Buck Owens
Merle Haggard
Jeannie C. Riley
Roy Acuff
George Jones
Ernest Tubb
Hank Williams
Waylon Jennings
Bill Monroe
Loretta Lynn
Patsy Cline
The Carter Family
Johnny Cash
Willie Nelson

Tammy Wynette
Kitty Wells
Floyd Tillman
Jimmie Rodgers
Kris Kristofferson

Floyd Tillman, author of "Slippin' Around."

ANSWERS

1. Roy Acuff	**12.** George Jones
2. Bill Monroe	**13.** Buck Owens
3. Willie Nelson	**14.** Merle Haggard
4. Tammy Wynette	**15.** Jeannie C. Riley
5. Ernest Tubb	**16.** Floyd Tillman
6. The Carter Family	**17.** Jimmie Rodgers
7. Loretta Lynn	**18.** Kitty Wells
8. Johnny Cash	**19.** Patsy Cline
9. Dolly Parton	**20.** Kris Kristofferson
10. Bobby Bare	**21.** Red Foley
11. Hank Williams	**22.** Waylon Jennings

YOU'RE SO COLD I'M TURNIN' BLUE

My mother was brought up to be a Southern Lady, a state of being that is sometimes as difficult to achieve as is the attainment of Nirvana, because one must master so many subtleties and nuances of behavior and speech. As a child, for example, I was taught never to use the word "woman" in referring to members of my own sex. Although this was never really explained, I soon learned that "woman" referred to an inferior species; my friends were always "ladies" or "girls."

Southern culture has thousands of such euphemisms and circumlocutions, most of which, I suspect, stem from the requirements of courtesy. In any event, Southerners thus nurtured a love for word games, and especially for similes, metaphors, and plain old puns, all of which allow the speaker to say what he or she means in an indirect manner. This, combined with a love for the tall tale, produced some of the most colorful language in America, some of the best examples of which are to be found in the titles of country songs. Here are some of my favorites.

"It's a 10–33 (Let's Get Jesus on the Line)"
"If Drinkin' Don't Kill Me (Her Memory Will)"
"Somebody Somewhere (Don't Know What He's Missin' Tonight)"
"While He's Makin' Love (I'm Makin' Believe)"
"If You Don't Quit Checkin' on Me (I'm Checkin' Out on You)"
"She Never Met a Man (She Didn't Like)"
"Pregnant Again"
"Don't Boogie Woogie (When You Say Your Prayers Tonight)"
"All I Want From You (Is Away)"
"Cheatin' on a Cheater"
"You're the One That Taught Me How to Swing"
"Excuse Me (I Think I've Got a Heartache)"
"If You Could Just Remember (What I Can't Forget)"
"Ride 'Em, Jewboy"
"My Quadroon"
"Out of My Head and Back in My Bed"
"To Make a Long Story Short (She's Gone)"
"In the Good Ole Days (When Times Were Bad)"
"Your Squaw's on the Warpath Tonight"

"It Ain't Fair (That It Ain't Right)"
"Muscatel Memories"
"I Gotta Get Drunk"
"She's Huggin' You (But She's Lookin' at Me)"
"Elvis Has Left the Building"
"Divorce or Destroy"
"I Think I'll Just Stay Here and Drink"
"There's Nobody Home on the Range Anymore"
"Stand on My Own Two Knees"
"I Still Hold Her Body (But I Think I've Lost Her Mind)"
"If You Loved a Liar (You'd Hug My Neck)"
"Get Your Biscuits in the Oven and Your Buns in the Bed"
"Who Put All My Ex's in Texas?"
"Pick Me Up on Your Way Down"
"For Better or Worse (But Not for Long)"
"If I Said You Had a Beautiful Body (Would You Hold It Against Me)"

"Your Wife's Been Cheatin' on Us Again"
"She's Actin' Single (I'm Drinkin' Doubles)"
"I'm the Only Hell My Mama Ever Raised"
"She's Everybody's Woman, I'm Nobody's Man"
"Big Balls in Cow Town"
"He's Got Nothing on Me But You"
"(A Man Can Be a Drunk Sometimes But) A Drunk Can't Be a Man"
"She Still Comes Around (To Love What's Left of Me)"
"Don't Come Home A-Drinkin' (With Lovin' on Your Mind)"
"Two Story House"
"(When Your Phone Don't Ring) It'll Be Me"
"If I Lay Down the Bottle Would You Lay Back Down With Me"
"I Just Started Hatin' Cheatin' Songs Today"
"Pass Me By (If You're Only Passin' Through)"
"Long Walk Off a Tall Rock"

DAY JOBS

"**D**on't give up your day job" is the first piece of advice given to every would-be country musician—very few are able to leave home and enter the business successfully without some kind of alternate financial support to see them through the difficult breaking-in period. In other cases, established country stars have parlayed their careers as musicians into careers in other businesses. Match the star with his or her "day job."

1.	Textile workers	LuluBelle Wiseman
2.	Cabin boy	George Jones
3.	Opera singer/voice teacher	Gene Autry
4.	North Carolina state representative	Montana Slim
5.	Sign painter	Rosanne Cash
6.	Auto assembly-line worker	Kris Kristofferson
7.	Fertilizer salesman	Lester Flatt and Earl Scruggs
8.	Drama teacher	David Allan Coe
9.	Semi-pro baseball player	Glen Campbell
10.	Bull rider	Willie Nelson
11.	Shoeshine boy/peanut salesman	Freddy Fender
12.	Used car salesman	Jeannie C. Riley
13.	Disc jockeys	Marshall Chapman
14.	Peace Corps worker	Merle Haggard
15.	Waitress	Tammy Wynette
16.	Governor of Louisiana	Jimmie Rodgers
17.	Railroad brakeman	Bill Anderson
18.	Bible salesman	Cliff Carlisle
19.	House painter	Hank Snow
20.	High school English teacher	Roy Acuff

21. Beautician
22. Secretary
23. Cowboy
24. Dishwasher
25. Actress
26. Mechanic
27. Convict
28. Garbage truck driver
29. Telegraph operator
30. Janitor
31. Debutante

Roger Miller
Lacy J. Dalton
J. D. Mainer
Vernon Dalhart
Kinky Friedman
Donna Fargo
Minnie Pearl
Billy Joe Shaver
Jerry Clower
Hank Williams
Jimmie Davis
Waylon Jennings

ANSWERS

1. Lester Flatt and Earl Scruggs
2. Hank Snow
3. Vernon Dalhart
4. LuluBelle Wiseman
5. Cliff Carlisle
6. J. D. Mainer
7. Jerry Clower
8. Minnie Pearl
9. Roy Acuff
10. Roger Miller
11. Hank Williams
12. Billy Joe Shaver
13. Waylon Jennings and Bill Anderson
14. Kinky Friedman
15. Lacy J. Dalton
16. Jimmie Davis

17. Jimmie Rodgers
18. Willie Nelson
19. George Jones
20. Donna Fargo
21. Tammy Wynette
22. Jeannie C. Riley
23. Montana Slim
24. Merle Haggard
25. Rosanne Cash
26. Freddy Fender
27. David Allan Coe
28. Glen Campbell
29. Gene Autry
30. Kris Kristofferson
31. Marshall Chapman

WORDS TO LIVE BY

Long before pop psychologists were telling us how to be our own best friends, country songwriters were dispensing advice about life for the price of a song. Here are some examples, all taken from the titles of country songs.

1. Act naturally.
2. Are you sure Hank done it this way?
3. Death is only a dream.
4. Don't be cruel.
5. Don't come home a-drinkin' with lovin' on your mind.
6. Don't fence me in.
7. Don't let your babies grow up to be cowboys.
8. Don't let your deal go down.
9. Don't make me go to bed and I'll be good.
10. Don't make me pregnant.
11. Don't rob another man's castle.
12. Don't take your love to town.
13. Forever is a long, long time.
14. If you've got the money, I've got the time.
15. It was always so easy to find an unhappy woman.
16. It wasn't God who made honky tonk angels.
17. Keep on the sunny side of life.
18. Let old Mother Nature have her way.
19. Life has its little ups and downs.
20. Mind your own business.
21. Move it on over.
22. Nothing's cold as ashes after the fire is gone.
23. Stand by your man.
24. There's more pretty girls than one.
25. Touch your woman.
26. Wealth won't save your soul.
27. We're getting closer to the grave each day.
28. We'll understand it better bye and bye.
29. What would you give in exchange for your soul?
30. When you're hot, you're hot.
31. You always hurt the one you love.
32. You've got to walk that lonesome valley.

Sterling
RECORDS, INC.
NEW YORK, N. Y.

204 A

WEALTH WON'T SAVE YOUR SOUL
(Hank Williams)
HANK WILLIAMS
And The Country Boys
Singing by
HANK WILLIAMS

THE GRAND TOUR

I'm going to assume that you are so excited about country music by now that you are ready for the ultimate: the Pilgrimage to Nashville, Tennessee, Music City, U.S.A., and home of the Grand Ole Opry. Time was when the Grand Old Opry shows on Friday and Saturday nights were the *only* reason to visit Nashville. Every weekend, rain or shine, men, women, old people, soldiers, little kids, and everybody else you might imagine lined up for blocks on Fifth Avenue North in front of the old Ryman Auditorium. They'd drive for miles and wait for hours to see country music's most famous show.

And in a slightly different manner, people still do today. Now, however,

the Opry is just one of lots of tourist attractions in Nashville. During the past ten years the citizens of the Athens of the South have wised up to the fact that all those people who come to see the Opry bring along plenty of money for other things too, and Nashville is now loaded with motels, restaurants, souvenir shops, tour buses, and the like, all promoted by a country music–conscious Chamber of Commerce. Therefore, I've outlined a four-

day visit to Nashville that includes a visit to
the Opry and also allows time to see both
country and noncountry sights in and around
Nashville.

Although the Opry is still the major attraction for the country music tourist, the
modern version, located in a big new Opry
House on the grounds of the Opryland, U.S.A.
amusement park, isn't nearly as funky as the
old Opry. Still, it's a pretty good show if you
haven't seen it before, and any trip to
Nashville must include an Opry visit.

For this reason, you ought to plan your
trip as far ahead of time as possible. A year
ahead isn't too soon to send for your tickets.
In January 1982, for example, I called to see
about the availability of Saturday night Opry
tickets for the following summer, and was told
that all Saturday night reserved seats for the
dates between March 20 and October 23,
1982, were sold. A few Friday night seats were

Music City meets the Athens of the South:
Loretta Lynn at Nashville's Parthenon.
Right: *The Nashville skyline.*

available, as were seats for Friday, Saturday, and Sunday matinees (the last show is staged only during the summer season). One can occasionally pick up a general admission Opry ticket during the week immediately before the show, but it's not wise to count on it.

Since Nashville is at its best from early spring to mid-October, it's best to plan your trip for sometime during this period. After you've read this, send for your Opry tickets immediately. Here's how:

Opry tickets cost $8 for reserved seats on Friday and Saturday for all people over three years of age. Friday, Saturday, and Sunday matinees cost $6. General admission tickets, priced at $7 for evening shows and $4 for matinees, go on sale every Tuesday before the weekend shows. These tickets must be bought in person. To order reserved seats, send a check or money order for the correct amount, along with a note stating the date you want tickets for (and alternate dates if your first choice isn't available) to: Opry Tickets, 2808 Opryland Drive, Nashville, Tennessee, 37214. No telephone orders are accepted; nor are credit cards.

Once this is done, you can relax for a while. When you get time, write to the Nashville Chamber of Commerce, 161 Fourth Avenue North, Nashville, Tennessee 37219 (or telephone 615-259-3900), and ask for tourist bro-chures, a list of local hotels, motels, and restaurants, and, most important, a good map of Nashville. It is impossible to navigate Nashville without a map; even with one it's fairly hard to get around. I don't mean to put a wet blanket on things, but Nashville has one of the highest per-capita auto accident rates in America, so study your maps before you go and develop at least a general idea of how to get from one place to another. Then, drive carefully.

I'm going to assume you've gotten your Opry tickets and made your Nashville hotel reservations. If you plan the basic four-day Nashville trip, this is all you have to do. If you have a longer vacation, say ten or twelve days, there are other interesting country music tourist spots in the states immediately surrounding Tennessee, which you may also want to visit. In addition, there are just some very pretty places you might want to see on your way. To that end, I'm including three different routes to Nashville, each of which should take four or five days in addition to the four days you spend in Nashville. Two of the trips will take you to Nashville from the northeast; the third approaches Nashville from the southwest. Finally, I've listed a few other spots in America you might want to hit, depending on where you're coming from. So let's go!

GETTING TO NASHVILLE THREE DIFFERENT WAYS

TRIP A:
Southwest from Lexington, Kentucky.

Before going: Make Nashville reservations. Reserve room and dinner at Boone Tavern.

Reserve room at Dupont Lodge. (See end of section for addresses.)

Day 1: Plan to arrive in Lexington, Kentucky, by 10 a.m. Spend most of your day visiting the Kentucky Horse Park, where you can see the Thoroughbred Horse Museum; visit the school where future horse farm workers are trained; see live examples of various breeds of horses; go on a trail ride; see a daily horse show; and picnic on the grounds. The horse park is not to be missed.

At about 3 p.m., leave the horse park, drive back to Interstate 75. Head south, and arrive in Berea, Kentucky, and check in at the Boone Tavern Hotel. Your dinner reservations should have been made in advance, so go to your room, change into something fresh, and prepare to eat one of the best dinners you've ever experienced. There's Kentucky spoon bread, fried chicken, fresh rolls, fruit, all kinds of vegetables, and apple pie for dessert. After dinner, go back to your room and sleep it off. This restaurant is guaranteed (by me) to put you in eaters' heaven. I want to be there right now!

Day 2: Spend your morning sightseeing around Berea, a small town that is home to Berea College. The college was founded before the Civil War as an Abolitionist school, and today dedicates itself to educating young people from Appalachia. Berea is loaded with shops that sell real mountain crafts, all expertly made, and some of the most beautiful quilts you've ever seen (expensive) are at stores just a block away from the Boone Tavern. You can find all kinds of folk songbooks and old-time records at the Council of the Southern Mountains Bookstore, and you'll want to buy baby blankets, place mats, and table cloths at Churchill Weavers on the college campus. In fact, you should keep a tight rein on your purse strings in Berea, because you won't have anything to spend in Nashville if you don't.

Leaving Berea around noon, return to Interstate 75 and drive south for about an hour and a half through the rolling hills with views of the mountains to come in the distance. If you want, stop at Renfro Valley (the exit is marked) and visit the home of John Lair's

Renfro Valley Barndance, a show that has been going strong every weekend since 1940 and which produced Red Foley, among other great country stars. Mr. Lair has a small country music museum on the grounds, and while you won't get to see an actual barn dance show, the museum is interesting. Return to Interstate 75 and drive south to the exit for Cumberland Falls. From here, you will take a very curvy highway, U.S. 25W, for about a half hour through the countryside and into the forests that surround Cumberland Falls State Park, one of the most spectacular of all Kentucky's parks.

Check in at the Dupont Lodge, the rustic-looking hotel that sits high on a hill above the Cumberland River, sometime between 2 and 3 o'clock. Since you will have made reservations in advance, go to your room, or to your private cabin (both are available, and the cabins have limited cooking facilities), change, and drive or, better, walk the short distance down the hill to see the falls, where the river falls almost a hundred feet into a spot called "the Devil's Bathtub." The falls are noted as being one of only two places in the world where a silver "moonbow" appears over the river on clear, moonlit nights. (The other place is in Africa, so you'll really be seeing a sight.)

Since you should eat dinner in the Dupont Lodge dining room about 6, don't venture on any of the park's numerous hiking trails today. Spend the rest of the afternoon walking about the area around the falls and drop in at the gift shop if you want. Return to the lodge and try the nightly buffet. Although not as good as the meal you will have had at Boone Tavern, the food at the falls is good, and there's plenty of it. After dinner you might want to join the square dance held each night in a pavilion hard by the lodge. Don't worry if you haven't square-danced before, because the staff will teach you, and even children can join in on the simple dances. If there's a moon out, go back to the falls and look at the moonbow. It's quite romantic.

Kentucky artisans. **Above left:** *dollmaker Noah Kinney;* **below left:** *painter Charlie Kinney;* **above:** *a quiltmaker in eastern Kentucky.*

Day 3: Depending on how much time you have, either spend the day and night at Cumberland Falls, or take the whole day for a leisurely drive to Nashville, which is 6 or 7 hours away.

If you stay at the falls, you can swim in the Olympic-sized pool, trail ride, take a river rafting trip, or hike along the dozens of trails in the park, either alone or with a guide, who'll tell you about the trees, flowers, and birds along the way. One especially nice trail, although a *very* difficult one, begins just on the other side of the bridge across the river in McCreary County. This trail will take you up a very steep path to the top of the mountain above the falls, and to a breathtaking view. If you can go a little further, you'll find Eagle Falls, a small but very pretty waterfall that is just below the big falls. Don't take this trail alone—wear stout shoes and take a canteen if you have one, because you'll be thirsty by the time you get all the way up the trail.

If you decide to spend the day driving, eat breakfast at Dupont Lodge and stop at a grocery to buy the makings of a picnic for later in the day—there will be lots of places for one along the road to Nashville. Cross the bridge over the river and drive for a few miles until you see the turnoff for Kentucky 90 on your left. This road is curvy but very pretty, and after about twenty miles connects with U.S. 27 south at Parker's Lake, Kentucky. Just south of Parker's Lake, a marked road to your right will take you to Natural Arch, a spectacular rock bridge in the middle of the Daniel Boone National Forest. Natural Arch is well equipped for picnics and weenie roasts, and there are plenty of hiking trails, including one rather difficult one that will take you to the very top of the arch, which is one of my favorite places in the world.

After visiting the arch, go back to U.S. 27 and drive south for another twenty or so miles, past Whitley City, Kentucky, to Pine Knot. You can tell you're there because there's a flashing yellow light at a wide intersection. Turn left and visit Kentucky Hills Industries, a mountain craft cooperative where you'll find wonderful examples of pottery, woodworking, weaving, sculpture, and needlework, all made by members of the co-op. Items from Kentucky Hills Industries were chosen by buyers at Bloomingdale's department store in New York City, for sale in the store's "Oh! Kentucky" promotion in 1981. You can buy the stuff for much less at its source.

Back on U.S. 27, go south for another fifteen miles across the Kentucky-Tennessee border to Oneida, Tennessee. Here, take

Tennessee 154 west to Jamestown and U.S. 127. This is a very pretty drive through gentle mountain terrain, so take your time and enjoy it. An alternate, curvier route, Tennessee 52 west to Jamestown (this road is just a bit south of 154) will take you through Rugby and Armathwaite, Tennessee, two towns founded by English settlers very early in the state's history. Parts of Rugby have been restored and are very picturesque.

At Jamestown, you can drive north on 127 a few miles to Pickett State Park, where you can picnic and have a swim in a dammed-up creek with lifeguards in attendance. There are restrooms and places for the kids to play, and even a campground should you want to spend the night. If not, take 127 south and head for Nashville. This is not a very pretty road, as it takes you mainly over flatland, but it's relatively straight and will connect at Crossville, Tennessee, with Interstate 40. From there it's a straight shot to Music City, U.S.A., so turn on your CB, if you have one, put some country music on the radio, and relax for a couple of hours.

Be sure to have your map of Nashville out by the time you get to the Mt. Juliet exit, so you'll be able to find your motel. Check in, have dinner, and get some rest before beginning your four-day tour of the city.

TRIP B:
Southwest from Lexington, Kentucky.

Before going: Make Nashville reservations. Reserve room at Pleasant Hill Inn as far in advance as possible. Make reservations for lunch at Beaumont Inn a couple of days in advance or upon arriving at Pleasant Hill. Make reservations in Cave City at one of the chain motels, such as the Holiday Inn or Ramada Inn, just to be sure. See end of this section for addresses.

Day 1: Plan to arrive in Lexington, Kentucky, by 10 a.m. and spend the day at the Kentucky Horse Park, described in Day 1 of Trip A. Leave around 3 p.m. and take U.S. 68 south through the bluegrass to Pleasant Hill, which is called Shakertown locally. Shakertown is the home of one of the last groups of people who followed the Shaker religion (named thus because the participants danced or "shook" during religious ceremonies), which died out in the early part of this century. The Shaker code prohibited marriage, and men and women stayed strictly apart; the buildings at Shakertown even have separate staircases for each. Pleasant Hill, which has been restored, contains the stone barns and dormitories the Shakers used, furnished completely with the austere, almost modern furniture they made. It's quite a pretty little place in the country, and the Inn at Pleasant Hill, though small, is one of the nicest spots in Kentucky to have a very superior dinner and spend the night. Make your reservations well in advance, because rooms are limited.

Day 2: Have breakfast at the Inn and spend a couple of hours afterward touring the buildings of Shakertown or just relaxing in the country. Leave Pleasant Hill around 11 a.m. and follow U.S. 68 south to Harrodsburg, one of the first settlements in Kentucky. Have lunch at the Beaumont Inn, another of the places in Kentucky where you'll find great Southern cooking in an antebellum setting. After lunch, you may want to visit Fort Harrod, where settlers barricaded themselves against hostile Indians, and the starting point for the later town of Harrodsburg. The fort is especially interesting for children. After visiting the fort, take U.S. 127 north for a few miles to the spot where it connects with the Bluegrass Parkway, a toll road that winds west to Elizabethtown through gentle hills and green countryside. You might want to make a brief stop at Bardstown, where you can visit the house that Stephen Foster wrote about in "My

Old Kentucky Home," Kentucky's state song, and also the Museum of Whiskey History, dedicated to bourbon whiskey, one of the state's most famous products. Buy some Bourbon Balls, chocolate-covered candies spiced with bourbon. They're good! After Bardstown, proceed west to Elizabethtown and Interstate 65, which will take you south toward Nashville.

From Elizabethtown it's only an hour or so's drive to Cave City, the entry point for Mammoth Cave National Park. Mammoth Cave is one of the largest underground caverns in the United States, and it's a sight you'll never forget. Check into your motel—there are several branches of nationally franchised motel chains in the immediate vicinity—have dinner, and get some rest.

Day 3: Spend the day touring Mammoth Cave. The tours are conducted by national park staff members, and you can choose to spend anywhere from two hours to all day underground in a world of stalactites and stalagmites and blind catfish and glass-bottomed boats. Box lunches are available for the all-day tours.

After coming back to the real world, take Interstate 65 south and head directly for Nashville. The trip from Cave City should take no more than two hours along this rather pleasant stretch of highway. Have your map of Nashville out by the time you reach Goodlettsville, Tennessee, so you can find your motel. Check in, have dinner, and rest up for the four-day tour of the city.

TRIP C:
Northeast from Fort Worth.

Before going: Make reservations in Nashville, Fort Worth, Hot Springs, Arkansas, and Memphis, Tennessee. *A Texas tip:* Buy a copy of *Texas Monthly* magazine and consult the guide at the beginning of the magazine for sights, restaurants, museums, and so on. See addresses at end of this section.

Day 1: Plan to arrive in Fort Worth, Texas, a.k.a. Cowtown, U.S.A., no later than 5 p.m. Fort Worth has lots of motels and hotels, and you can get lists by writing the Chamber of Commerce. Check in at your motel, change clothes, and head for Theo's Saddle and Sirloin Inn at 120 Exchange Place, near the famous Fort Worth stockyards. Have a real Texas steak and some homemade bread. Follow that with some fresh apple ice cream. Rest a minute or two.

Then head for Billy Bob's Texas at 2520 North Commerce, which is not far away. Billy Bob's vies with Gilley's club in Houston for being the world's largest honky tonk, and besides fine country music, you can see *live* bullriding under the sprawling roof, which covers about forty separate bar stations; a V.I.P. room, where you can see the actual eyepatch John Wayne wore in the movie *True Grit*, clothes shops, dance floors—you name it. Billy Bob's is open until 2 a.m., so pace yourself. Be sure you know how to find your way back to your motel.

Day 2: Try to get up and have breakfast. If you're still all there after the night at Billy Bob's, redeem yourself by visiting the Amon Carter Museum of Western Art at 1300 Montgomery. Here you will see some beautiful paintings by Frederic Remington as well as works by lesser-known western artists.

Leave Fort Worth between noon and 2 p.m. and head east on Interstate 30 for Hot Springs, Arkansas. It will take you about four or five hours to get to this mountain spa in the hills of Arkansas, located not far off the Interstate. Check in at your motel or hotel, have dinner, and get some rest.

Day 3: Spend the morning touring Hot Springs. You might even want to avail yourself of a bath at one of the town's numerous bathhouses. Relax until around 2 p.m., and then hit the Interstate again. Head east to

Memphis, check in at your motel, and have dinner.

Day 4: This is your Elvis Presley Day. Take a Gray Line tour of places that are connected with Elvis' life—like Humes High School—and visit Elvis' grave at Graceland.

Buy Elvis souvenirs at stores all along Elvis Presley Boulevard. Leave Memphis around 5 or 6 p.m. and take Interstate 40 east to Nashville. The drive will take about three hours. Check in at your Nashville motel and rest up for your four-day tour of the city.

COUNTRY MUSIC SIGHTS IN NEARBY STATES

ALABAMA

In Montgomery, Hank Williams fans all try to visit Hank's grave. The trouble is, it's a little hard to find. The grave is located in the Oakwood Cemetery Annex, which isn't marked; in fact, the cemetery isn't even listed in the Montgomery telephone book. So here's what to do. First find Montgomery's main police station, which is located in the Montgomery Public Affairs Building—Oakwood Cemetery is right beside that building. Have the cemetery attendant show you where to turn for the annex, and after the entry, take the first right and go as far as you can. Turn left. Keep driving until you see Hank's grave. It's a very large stone, with the words "I saw the light" on its face and a stone cowboy hat at its base. The grave faces the woods at the back of the cemetery.

The only other Hank Williams memorabilia to be found in Montgomery are in a trophy case located in the State Department of Archives and History Building on the grounds of the Alabama State Capitol. In this case you will see two of Hank's suits, five hats, a portrait, and some sheet music. That's it.

KENTUCKY

If you're a Loretta Lynn fan and have read the book or seen the movie *Coal Miner's*

Daughter, you probably want to know if you can visit the real Loretta Lynn birthplace. It's awfully rough country and it's hard to find, but you can get there. This side trip will cost you an extra day, but if you really want to visit Butcher Hollow, here's how.

From Lexington, Kentucky, take Interstate 64 east to Winchester, where the Interstate intersects with the Bert Combs Mountain Parkway (a toll road). Follow the parkway east to Salyersville, then take U.S. 460 east to Paintsville. At Paintsville, follow U.S. 23 south about ten or fifteen miles to Van Lear. These are curvy roads, so drive slowly. At Van Lear, which is merely a clearing in the road, you will see a very large building, which was the old coal company headquarters, on your left (watch closely or you'll miss it). Across from this building is a cemetery. Turn left here and go straight up the hill on a blacktop road, which soon turns to dirt. Keep going on the dirt road until you see a store on your right. This is old company store Number Five, which is now called Webb's Grocery and is run by Loretta Lynn's brother, Herman Webb. Stop at the store and have a Coke and a Moon Pie and talk to Herman. He's a very quiet, shy man, so you won't have much of a conversation, but he'll tell you how to get the rest of the way to the holler, which you'll need to know

Flowers at Hank's grave.

her cousin Dixie, located even further up another dirt road past the house. Most cars can't make the trip to Dixie's, and if you want to go there, it will be a hard, dusty, long walk. I'd suggest that you not try to go further into the hollow unless you're an intrepid outdoorsman.

After you've visited the house, go back to Herman's store and have another soft drink, which you'll need after riding the dusty road. Plan to spend the night in Paintsville or Prestonburg, which is located a few miles south of Paintsville on U.S. 23.

From Prestonburg, you can follow Kentucky 80 southeast to Hazard. Here, take the Daniel Boone Parkway (a toll road) southeast to London, Kentucky. At London, either take Interstate 75 south to Knoxville and Interstate 40 west to Nashville or take the Cumberland Parkway (a toll road) west to Glasgow and Interstate 65 south to Nashville.

MISSISSIPPI

In Meridian, the birthplace of Jimmie Rodgers, there is a small Jimmie Rodgers museum and memorial in Meridian's city park. The folks in Meridian seem to be a whole lot more aware of their local hero than do the people in Montgomery, Alabama, be-

even with these directions. Follow the dirt road on past Herman's store as far as your car will go (it'll be easier if you have four-wheel drive). Loretta's old homeplace, which looks exactly as it looked in the movie of her life, will eventually appear on your right, set about halfway up the hill and surrounded by rambling roses. The people who now live in the house are distant relatives of Loretta and are usually very friendly. They'll take you through the house—a small one—and perhaps try to sell you a few Loretta Lynn souvenirs.

This house is only the place where Loretta Lynn grew up. The house where she was born is now a storage shed on a place owned by

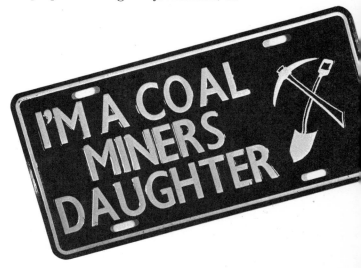

Elvis and the Colonel at Graceland, with Elvis' new color TV.

cause almost every year for the past nine years, the city has hosted a week-long Jimmie Rodgers Memorial Festival, complete with dances, appearances by tóp country entertainers, a barbeque, talent contests, and a parade. The festival usually takes place in early summer. For information on this year's event, write to the Country Music Association, P.O. Box 22299, Nashville, Tennessee 37202.

In Tupelo, not too far southeast of Memphis, you can visit Elvis Presley's birthplace. The small wood frame house has been extensively restored and refurnished since the Presley family lived there; Tupelo natives say the original home was much more humble than what you see today. Tupelo also is the site of the Presley Memorial Chapel, erected by Elvis' fans. The house and chapel are located at 306 Elvis Presley Drive.

TENNESSEE

In other times, Memphis was known as the birthplace of the blues, and Beale Street was where all the tourists went. Today Memphis is known as Elvis Presley's adopted hometown, and all the tourists go to visit Graceland, his mansion, and on its grounds, his grave. Located at 3764 Elvis Presley Boulevard, the house is now open, in part, to the public. You can see Elvis' TV room, his music room, his pool room, and his carport, among other things; and outside, you can visit the graves of Elvis and his family.

It's advisable to make reservations in advance for this tour, which costs $5 for adults and $3 for children. To do this, you can call 1-800-238-2000 (toll free) up to six months in advance. Mail orders should be addressed to Graceland Enterprises, P.O. Box 16508, Memphis, Tennessee 38116.

Checks, money orders, Visa, Mastercard, and American Express are accepted.

Across the street from the house and all along Elvis Presley Boulevard are stores, restaurants and dozens of souvenir shops, all of which claim some connection with Elvis. In fact, it's not unusual to find stray members of Elvis' "Memphis Mafia"—the group of men friends with whom he surrounded himself— hanging out in one of these establishments. Some hawk copies of their "memoirs" about Elvis.

The Gray Line conducts bus tours of Elvis-related sights in Memphis, including Sun Studios, where he, Johnny Cash, Jerry Lee Lewis, Charlie Rich, and Carl Perkins first recorded. It might be advisable to take the Gray Line tour first and mark down the places that look good so that you can visit them later. Call 345-8687 for reservations and information.

TEXAS

In Carthage, you can visit Jim Reeves' gravesite, which is located in a memorial park just outside town. Reeves' widow, Mary Reeves Davis, has announced plans to build a Jim Reeves museum on the site as well. To find Carthage, travel Interstate 20 to Longview, Texas, turn onto U.S. 59 south, and drive about 20 miles to Carthage. The town is very small, so the Reeves grave is easy to find.

If you want to go to Luckenbach, you won't find Willie and Waylon and the boys, as the song says, but you will find a pretty little spot beside the river that is just fine for a picnic. Luckenbach also has a general store, but that's all. To get to Luckenbach, follow U.S. 290 west from Austin. Pass through Johnson City and stop by the LBJ park just outside town to see longhorn steer and bison. Then follow the road to tiny Stonewall, and drive a few more miles until you see the turnoff for ranch road 1376 on your left. Follow that road to the place where it forms a crossroad and you'll be in Luckenbach.

Most people think that Gilley's, the humongous nightclub immortalized in the movie *Urban Cowboy*, is in Houston. It's not. It's in

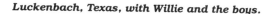

Luckenbach, Texas, with Willie and the boys.

the Houston suburb of Pasadena, which is east of Houston, on state road 225 off loop 610. The specific address is 4500 Spencer Highway. Gilley's and Billy Bob's in Fort Worth are constantly vying for the title of "world's biggest honky tonk." While Billy Bob's has the edge at this writing, Mickey Gilley is planning to add a bit more room to his place so he can regain the title. Anyhow, both places are too big to be imagined. At Gilley's you can dance, ride the mechanical bull, play with the mechanical punching bag, drink Gilley Beer,

watch live country music by top acts, play any of the acres of video and pinball games, and probably get involved in any of the several fights that seem to be going on at any one time. Not to worry, though, Gilley's security is good. The club is open seven days a week from 10 a.m. until 2 a.m.

One of the world's largest honky tonks—the dance floor at Gilley's Club.

THE FOUR-DAY MUSIC CITY WHING DINGER

This is the basic tour of Nashville. Since you're going to see the Opry on Friday or Saturday, plan to arrive in town either late Wednesday night or early Thursday morning. Be sure to have all your reservations— Opry tickets, motel, and so forth—in order before you leave home. Your motel should

cost between $20 and $50 a night, depending on where you stay. Since you will need to pay admission to some places and will want to buy souvenirs at others, I'd suggest that each adult take about a hundred dollars in spending money for the four-day stay, more if you plan to eat at a fancy restaurant or visit any nightclubs. This may sound like a lot, but you can always take it home with you if you don't spend it all. Canadian money is accepted at many places, and your hotel staff will assist you in changing it if necessary.

DETAILS

Day 1 (Thursday): You should start your country music vacation by orienting yourself to Nashville and its sights, and the best way to do this is to choose a Gray Line tour package. Nashville has several other competing tour companies, but Gray Line is the most thorough and its guides are reliable. The company offers several different packages, but I suggest you take the "Discover Music City" tour, which leaves from 501 Broadway daily, year round, at 10 a.m. The price for this tour is $9.50 for adults and $4.75 for children. Call 244-7330 to make reservations and to confirm the fare.

On this tour you will drive past the homes of several stars, including those of Minnie Pearl, Webb Pierce, Porter Wagoner, and the late Hank Williams. The bus stops on Music Row, where there are lots of souvenir shops, and at the Country Music Hall of Fame, but you won't have enough time to visit all of these places during the tour. Note their locations and plan to return in the afternoon. The tour will also take you past several other non-country Nashville sights, such as the State Capitol, the old Ryman Auditorium, the Parthenon, and Fort Nashboro. The trip will take about three hours.

Afternoon. Plan to have lunch between 1 and 2 p.m. at one of the restaurants where music business people hang out: Faison's, Maude's Courtyard, or O'Charley's. These restaurants are moderately expensive ($10 or so a person), so you might prefer to grab a burger if your budget is limited. Then return to the Music Row area and visit the very best tourist attractions Nashville has to offer:

the Country Music Hall of Fame and Museum and Studio B. It's quite possible to spend the entire afternoon at these two places, so allow yourself plenty of time.

In the Hall of Fame, as it's called for short, you will see exhibits that are both educational and entertaining. There are exhibits depicting the history of country music's development, from mountain folk music and Southern gospel up through the present; films of country stars like Jimmie Rodgers and Bob Wills run continuously; display cases are stocked with stage clothes and memorabilia donated to the museum by country stars; and there is a whole room dedicated to the members of the Country Music Hall of Fame. In addition, there's a mock-up of the inside of a country star's touring bus, and there is Elvis Presley's "Solid Gold Cadillac"—the real thing.

The museum's "country store" offers the best souvenirs to be found in Nashville. The store stocks almost every book about country music that exists, hard-to-find records and songbooks, and all the country music magazines. There are also T-shirts, posters, and some of the nicest postcards you'll find anywhere. I suggest that you allocate the largest part of your souvenir budget to the store at the Hall of Fame, where you will find the best quality for your money.

As you enter the Hall of Fame, buy tickets for Studio B, a real recording studio (where folks like Elvis Presley actually made records), which has been donated to the museum. Studio B is a so-called "hands on" experience, because visitors are allowed to work the actual controls of the sound board as they learn how a record is made. You'll appreciate your own records much more after having learned how they were made, and you'll hear things on records that you never noticed before.

If you have any time left after seeing the Hall of Fame and Studio B, take a short walking tour of "Music Row," a few square blocks between Division Street and Grand

Avenue, where most of the nation's record companies have their Nashville branches. For the most part these are merely office buildings, but who knows who you might see going in and out of them? There are also several other tourist "sights" in this area, like the Country Music Wax Museum, just across Division Street from the Hall of Fame, and the Music Row Entertainment Center on 16th Avenue South.

You won't really miss anything if you skip these places, but most tourists don't, and it's certainly no sin to visit them.

Evening. Return to your motel or hotel around 6 p.m. and rest for a little while before dinner. Afterward you might find it fun to visit the Alamo, which is a western wear store at 324 Broadway. The Alamo's clothes are frankly gaudy—Dolly Parton might like them—but fun. Some of the clothes worn in the film *Coal Miner's Daughter* came from here. The store is open until 2 a.m.

If you're a nightclub type, Nashville has an area called Printer's Alley, which is located just off Church Street downtown. Printer's Alley clubs are mostly high-class strip joints, but Boots Randolph, of "Yakkety Sax" fame, has a club in the Alley and he appears there often. Another fixture of the Alley is a guy called "Skull," who works the doors of various places in the area. He gets his name from the fact that he has a belt buckle shaped in the form of a skull, and when he takes your money, the skull's eyes light up. If you're easily offended, however, I'd suggest that you steer clear of the Alley. Stay in your room and watch television instead.

Day 2 (Friday): If you have Opry tickets for Friday afternoon or night, plan to spend your day at Opryland and the afternoon or evening at the Opry.

Opryland is a large amusement park, which opened in 1971 as both a park and the site for the new Grand Ole Opry House.

It's huge and is open every day between Memorial Day and Labor Day and on weekends from early spring through late fall. To find it, take Interstate 40 east until it runs into Briley Parkway, and follow the signs from there. Opryland has rides, restaurants, petting zoos, gift shops, several musical revues that cover every kind of music from country to Broadway show tunes to rock and roll, and a museum inside the Opry House itself. It's quite easy to spend a whole day there— in fact, if you have children, they'll probably want to spend the whole four-day trip there. The park is clean and the food is edible if you don't eat too much of it. I'd suggest you limit yourself to one corny dog, one cotton candy, one bag of popcorn, one or two pieces of fried chicken, and no more than two guitar-shaped ice cream bars. Opryland's souvenirs are generally of good quality, but they can get expensive if you don't watch it.

My favorite Opryland attraction is a chicken

that will play tic tac toe with you for a quarter. This chicken is smart, friends! I've lost serious money to it, and I keep coming back for more. The chicken is located near the petting zoo, so don't get so fascinated with his game that you neglect to watch the goats, who will be trying to eat your clothes.

Eat an early dinner at Opryland and proceed directly to the Opry House on the grounds for the big show. The Opry is much changed from the old days in many respects, and purists feel that the institution no longer has validity, except as a kind of museum. True, most of the Opry's members are getting along in years, and true, the new Opry House is air-conditioned so that you don't get to use all those nice funeral parlor paper fans they used to sell outside the Ryman Auditorium, but the Opry is still fun. The show is certainly worth $8, since it lasts as long as four hours,

Exhibits at the Country Music Hall of Fame and Museum. Below: Elvis Presley's gold Cadillac at the Hall of Fame.

and you'll get to see lots of "living legends" like Roy Acuff, Minnie Pearl, Bill Monroe, and Ernest Tubb. You won't get to see younger performers like Waylon Jennings or Willie Nelson, but Dolly Parton appears at the Opry every once in a great while, as does Loretta Lynn whenever she's in town. See it one time in your life, at least.

After the show, you're going to be completely exhausted, so you'll probably feel like going straight back to your hotel. Sleep late on Saturday.

Alternative. If you don't have Friday night Opry tickets, you can spend Friday doing a little more sightseeing in Nashville and in the nearby town of Hendersonville. After breakfast, visit anything you may have missed on Music Row the day before, and then go to Ernest Tubb's Record Store at 417 Broadway. Tubb, or "the Texas Troubadour" as he's known popularly, started this record store back in the fifties, at a time when one couldn't find country music records in Nashville (the natives were apparently too snobbish to sell them). The store—and Tubb's branch store on Music Valley Drive near Opryland—still stocks the most complete selection of country music records to be found outside of collectors' sales. You can also buy nice Ernest Tubb souvenirs—get some Tubb potholders, they're quality items.

Tubb's Music Valley store is now the site of the weekly "Saturday Night Jamboree," the live radio broadcast that airs every Saturday night after the Opry. These days the Jamboree is usually hosted by Tubb's son, Justin, but if you're lucky enough to be in town on a night when the Troubadour himself is performing, be sure and go.

After visiting Ernest Tubb's, you might want to take a drive out Lebanon Pike (U.S. 70) to the Hermitage, Andrew Jackson's beautiful homeplace on Rachel's Lane. The house and its gardens are a national historic landmark.

If you're not in the mood for history, however, drive to Hendersonville to visit the Johnny Cash Museum and "Twitty City," the affectionate name for Conway Twitty's new museum and tourist attraction. Hendersonville is just northeast of Nashville on U.S. 31E, which you reach by taking Gallatin Avenue out of town.

The Johnny Cash Museum, souvenir shop, antique store, and House Of Cash, the Cash/Carter business offices, are open year-round. In the museum, you'll see things like the bed Johnny and his wife, June Carter, slept in when they were first married; the actual cross, robe, and crown of thorns worn by the man who played Jesus in Johnny's movie *Gospel Road;* and the handwritten manuscripts of Johnny's and June's autobiographies. There are also various souvenirs of U.S. history, and a restored L&N railroad depot. In the gift shop—where Johnny's relatives sometimes work—there are the usual souvenirs, as well as copies of books by Johnny and June. One of the most interesting features of this enterprise is a store called June's Antiques, where the visitor can buy " antiques and jewelry collected by June Carter Cash." Who knows? You might even see Johnny and June in person.

After visiting the Cash development, cross the road and visit Twitty City. Much more than a museum, this project is supposed to have "a town square reminiscent of the 19th Century" where there will be record, gift, and souvenir shops; picnic grounds; and houses for Conway and each of his four children. Visitors will be given guided tours of Conway's house.

In the late afternoon, drive back to Nashville, change clothes, and have a steak dinner at the Peddler. Not as fancy as Julian's, the Peddler still attracts a fair number of music-business types, if you know who to look for. Go to bed early on Friday night, because tomorrow you'll go to Opryland.

Day 3 (Saturday): Visit Opryland and the Opry (see description preceding); or follow the alternate plan for Friday if you saw Opryland yesterday.

Day 4 (Sunday): This is going to be a real "day in the country." Check out of your motel after breakfast, load up the car, and buy the makings of a big picnic (ask the motel clerk to give you directions to the store nearest you). Then get on Interstate 40 west and drive about 70 miles to the Waverly exit. Turn north on state road 13 and drive until you see the entrance for Loretta Lynn's Dude Ranch. Although I've just planned for you to spend one day here, if you have time, and if you have a camper or a tent, you can stay here overnight. There are all the facilities for campers, including hook-ups, a grocery store, showers, restrooms, and so forth. For information about this season's prices, write Loretta Lynn's Dude Ranch, Hurricane Mills, Tennessee 37078, or call 615-296-7700.

If you're just staying for the day, however, you'll still have a great time. First drive to the "town" of Hurricane Mills itself, so named because of a millhouse—which used to be known as "Anderson's Mill"—that still stands there. On the left side of the road, you'll see Loretta Lynn's house just as it appeared in *Coal Miner's Daughter* (many parts of the movie were filmed on the ranch). You can look at the house, but you can't go in. After looking at the house, turn right on the little bridge that spans the Duck River, and visit

Loretta's gift shop and museum, both of which are now housed in the Old Mill. The gift shop is standard Nashville fare, except that it's heavy with Loretta Lynn souvenirs. (Get a T-shirt that says "Nowhere else but Loretta Lynn's Dude Ranch.")

The museum is something else again. It's my next-to-favorite (after the Hall of Fame) in Nashville because it's so personal. Each of the exhibits, which include things like rocks Loretta picked up on visits to Butcher Holler, a red nightie given her by Patsy Cline, and many of Loretta's awards, is accompanied by a little index card written by Loretta herself. It's almost like being with Loretta, and you're sure to like it.

In addition to the gift shop and museum, there's also a western wear shop in Hurricane Mills, where some of Loretta's children occasionally work. The quality of the stock is good, and prices are high, but not prohibitive considering what you're buying. Ask anyone who works at the place to suggest a good spot for a picnic. I like a spot back down the road near the entrance, where one can sit under the trees near the stream. You can also join a trail ride, see some of Loretta's many animals, and take a swim in the pool if you pay a small fee. Check beforehand on this year's price by writing the above address or by calling from Nashville a couple of days ahead of time.

By now it'll be going on evening, and you should think about heading for home. Go back to Interstate 40 and head east or west, sure in the knowledge that you're now a Music City veteran. As they say in Nashville: "Y'all come back soon!"

FAN FAIR:
THE ABSOLUTE ULTIMATE
COUNTRY VACATION

If you can manage a vacation during the first week of June, disregard everything previously written about visiting Nashville, because that week is when Fan Fair—the country music fan's dream week—takes place. Sponsored by the Country Music Association and the Grand Ole Opry, Fan Fair has been going on for ten years and it's gotten so popular that it was moved to the Tennessee State Fairgrounds this year. It is, however, the best entertainment package available to country music fans anywhere.

In the summer of 1982, the registration price for Fan Fair was $50 per person (plus $8 per person for Opry tickets). For this you got: admission to shows featuring the artists of every major record label in Nashville—and there are enough to provide three days' worth of shows; barbecue prepared by the Chuckwagon Gang of Odessa, Texas; a celebrity softball tournament, featuring famous country musicians like Bill Anderson on the teams; special interest shows (bluegrass, Cajun, etc.); a great old-timer's reunion show; the grand master's fiddling contest; a big square dance; and, best of all, a chance to meet the stars in person at booths set up by their fan clubs. You want Loretta Lynn's autograph? You can get it—in person—at Fan Fair.

Fan Fair was first organized because the annual Disc Jockeys' Convention (CMA Week), which is held to coincide with the CMA Awards Show each October, had begun to get crowded with fans eager to see the stars. Thus little business got done, and as CMA Week is supposed to be an industry event, held to encourage good relations with people who run country music radio stations and to discuss the business affairs of the Country Music Association, Fan Fair was born—a whole week just for the fans. Even Friday and Saturday night Opry tickets are reserved that week for people who have registered for Fan

Fair (nonregistrants can still see Opry matinees on that weekend, however).

In past years Fan Fair was held at Nashville's Municipal Auditorium, and things could get a bit crazy because there were so many people (registration in 1981 was about 15,000). It was especially nutty in the vicinity of the fan club booths when the star appeared to sign autographs. No sooner was an announcement made on the public address system that one or another star had shown up to sign autographs, than the flimsy booths were stampeded with fans, pushing, shoving, hollering, and generally carrying on. It is hoped that the new location will solve this problem as well as the problem of overcrowding at record label shows.

Nonetheless, Fan Fair has always provided the fans with the best chance they'll ever get to meet stars in person, to see their favorites sing, and to get to know other people who share their interests. It's a guaranteed experience of a lifetime, and Nashville goes all-out to see that everyone has a good time.

Here's how to register. First, either call 615-889-7503, or write Fan Fair, 2804 Opryland Drive, Nashville 37214 for information on this year's dates and registration prices. Then send the required amount per person, plus the amount required for Opry tickets (state which night you prefer) to Fan Fair, 2804 Opryland Drive, Nashville 37214. It's good to register about six months ahead of time if you can, especially if you want Opry tickets. At the same time, write to the Nashville Chamber of Commerce, 161 Fourth Avenue, Nashville 37219 for a list of area motels. Make your reservations for rooms as soon as you have your Fan Fair registration assured. If you have a group of people who'd all like to visit Fan Fair together, the Opry tour service—Opryland Travel—has a limited number of tour packages for sale each year. For information write Opryland Travel, 2802 Opryland Drive, Nashville 37214.

Opposite: _Fan Fair fans eat the Chuckwagon Gang's barbecue._ **Below:** _Tammy Wynette's Silver Eagle—the country star's home on the range._

The only problem about visiting Fan Fair is that there is so much going on that you'll find it hard to make time to see other Nashville sights such as the Hall of Fame and the various star museums. One solution is to plan to take the first and last days of Fan Fair week for these sights or to plan to stay an extra day or two in Nashville. Then again, you can always visit Nashville next year.

USEFUL ADDRESSES

Alabama

Alabama Bureau of Publicity And
  Information
532 South Perry Street
Montgomery, Alabama 36130

Arkansas

Arkansas Department of Tourism
Little Rock, Arkansas 72201

Kentucky

Kentucky Department of Tourism
Capitol Plaza Tower
Frankfort, Kentucky 40601 (502-564-4930)

The Kentucky Horse Park
Route 6, Ironworks Pike
Lexington, Kentucky 40511 (606-233-4303)

Boone Tavern Hotel
Berea, Kentucky 40403 (606-986-9341)*

The Renfro Valley Barn Dance and Jamboree
Mount Vernon, Kentucky 40456 (606-256-2664)

Dupont Lodge
Cumberland Falls State Park
c/o Post Office
Corbin, Kentucky 40701 (606-528-4121)

The Daniel Boone National Forest
c/o Forest Supervisor
100 Vaught Road
Winchester, Kentucky 40391 (606-744-5656)

The Inn At Pleasant Hill (Shakertown)
Route 4
Harrodsburg, Kentucky 40330 (606-734-5411)*

The Beaumont Inn
Harrodsburg, Kentucky 40330 (606-734-3381)*

The Bardstown/Nelson County Tourist and
  Convention Commission
P.O. Box 614
Bardstown, Kentucky 40004 (502-348-9545)

Mammoth Cave National Park
Cave City, Kentucky 42259 (502-758-2328)

Mississippi

Mississippi Division of Tourism
Mississippi Department of Economic
  Development
P.O. Box 849
Jackson, Mississippi 39205 (1-800-647-2290)

Meridian Chamber of Commerce
P.O. Box 790
Meridian, Mississippi 39301 (601-693-1306)

Tupelo Community Development Foundation
P.O. Drawer A
Tupelo, Mississippi 38801 (601-842-4521)

*Jacket may be required for men at lunch and dinner

Tennessee

Tennessee Department of Tourist Development
601 Broadway, P.O. Box 23170
Nashville, Tennessee 37202 (615-741-2158)

Memphis:

Memphis Convention and Visitors Bureau
12 South Main, Suite 107
Memphis, Tennessee 38103 (901-526-1919)

Gray Line Of Memphis
3755 Elvis Presley Boulevard, #3
Memphis, Tennessee 38116 (901-345-8687)

Nashville:

Nashville Chamber of Commerce
161 Fourth Avenue North
Nashville, Tennessee 37219

Opry Tickets
2808 Opryland Drive
Nashville, Tennessee 37214

Fan Fair
2804 Opryland Drive
Nashville, Tennessee 37214 (615-889-7503)

Opryland Travel
2802 Opryland Drive
Nashville, Tennessee 37214

The Country Music Association
P.O. Box 22299
Nashville, Tennessee 37202

Gray Line Of Nashville
501 Broadway
Nashville, Tennessee 37203 (615-244-7330)

The Country Music Hall of Fame and Museum
4 Music Square East
Nashville, Tennessee 37203 (615-256-1639)

Ernest Tubb Record Shops
417 Broadway/Music Valley Drive
P.O. Box 500
Nashville, Tennessee 37202 (1-800-251-1904)

Boat Trip on the *Belle Carol* or
  Captain Ann
First Avenue North (off Broadway)
(615-356-4120)

The Johnny Cash Museum and House Of
  Cash
Box 508
Hendersonville, Tennessee 37075

The Conway Twitty Museum
Hendersonville, Tennessee 37075

Loretta Lynn's Dude Ranch
Hurricane Mills, Tennessee 37078
(615-296-7700)

Texas

Tourist Information
Texas State Highway Department
State Capitol
Austin, Texas 78701

POP QUIZ!

Here are ten frequently asked questions. Some are easy to answer; others are ob-scure. Answer as many as you can before checking the answers at the end of the section.

1. Why does Johnny Cash wear black?

2. What's the origin of the name "Grand Ole Opry"?

3. Why is country music so popular in Japan?

4. Who fixes Dolly Parton's hair?

5. What's Tootsie's Orchid Lounge?

6. What's the meaning of the radio call letters WSM? WLS?

7. What was the Wabash Cannon Ball?

8. Who was Luke the Drifter?

9. Was the film *Coal Miner's Daughter* really true?

10. Why did country bands begin using electric instruments?

Can you find Dolly's wig?

ANSWERS

1. Johnny Cash, who's nicknamed "the Man In Black" because he always wears black suits, first announced his purpose in adopting the color as his own on the 1971 album *Man In Black.* In the title song, Cash sings:

I wear the black for the poor and beaten down,
livin' on the hopeless hungry side of town.
I wear it for the prisoner who has long paid for his crime,
but is there because he's a victim of the time.
I wear black for those who've never read, or listened to the words that Jesus said . . .

The song continues with this roll call of victims: the sick, the lonely, the old, drug addicts, soldiers killed in Vietnam, and so forth, and concludes with the line: "I'll try to carry off a little darkness on my back. 'Til things are brighter, I'm the man in black." Cash has continued to wear only black in public since 1971, although he did sport a red, white, and blue embroidered eagle on his stage outfit during the U.S. Bicentennial in 1976.

2. The WSM Barn Dance changed its name to the "Grand Ole Opry" some time in the fall of 1927. The originator of the title is said to have been George D. Hay, a.k.a. "the Solemn Old Judge," who was in charge of the program for WSM, and who gave the program much of its flavor in the early days. In his book, *The Grand Ole Opry, The Early Years, 1925–35,* Charles K. Wolfe gives the following widely accepted account of the event:

Hay and the Opry cast were waiting for a network show, "The NBC Music Appreciation Hour," with noted conductor Walter Damrosch, to end so they could come on with the locally produced show. As he concluded, Damrosch made a comment about "there being no place

in the classics for realism" and conducted a short piece depicting a train ride. Hay, coming on seconds later, proclaimed ". . . from here on out for the next three hours we will present nothing but realism. It will be down to earth for the 'earthy'." He then introduced Deford Bailey who did *his* depiction of a train ride, "Pan American Blues." Afterwards, Hay said, "For the past hour we have been listening to music taken largely from Grand Opera, but from now on we will present the Grand Ole Opry."

There are a few people who doubt this account, but not many. It's been the Grand Ole Opry ever since.

3. Country music, along with some rock and roll music, is much favored by Japanese fans. Not only do the Japanese like American country stars and music, but they have a small country industry of their own—there's even a Japanese "Johnny Cash." It's probable that some of this popularity stems from a strange coincidence. During World War II, Tokyo Rose—the infamous female DJ (actually several women) who broadcast demoralizing messages to American troops each night— apparently played a lot of country music, because a lot of country music was sad. One popular song was Floyd Tillman's "Each Night at Nine," a song about how the soldier longed for home each night when he had to go to bed at 9 p.m. In any event, the Japanese seem to have listened to Tokyo Rose's broadcasts about as much as did the Americans. Country music's popularity among the Japanese boomed in the years after the war, and it's certain that Tokyo Rose had a lot to do with it.

4. Dolly Parton's "hair"—at least the wigs that you see whenever Dolly appears in public—has been cared for by her Aunt Coleen Owens, a graduate of the Knoxville (Tennessee) School of Beauty, since Dolly was about ten years old. Mrs. Owens now limits her employment to Dolly alone, and she has a fully equipped beauty shop in her basement at home in Nashville, where her only customers are Dolly's disembodied wigs. Aunt Coleen also travels with her niece from time to time, and the fact that Dolly's now a superstar with the wherewithal to hire anyone she wants to fix her hair hasn't altered her faith in Coleen Owens. Mrs. Owens says she also fiddles with Dolly's real hair—which is dark blond— from time to time. Dolly's wigs are synthetic, Aunt Coleen explains, because they're more

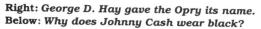

Right: *George D. Hay gave the Opry its name.*
Below: *Why does Johnny Cash wear black?*

durable and easier to wash than a human hair wig.

5. Tootsie's Orchid Lounge, the seedy historic beer joint across the alley from the back door of the Opry's old quarters at the Ryman Auditorium, still exists, but without Tootsie Bess, the much-loved proprietor who died of cancer February 18, 1978, there isn't much reason to go there. Tootsie, born Hattie Louise Tatum, ran a series of beer joints starting in 1941, and opened her most famous spot in 1961.

She was a friend to every musician— famous or infamous—who came to her door, and she willingly loaned money and donated free beer to people like Kris Kristofferson, Mel Tillis, Tom T. Hall, Willie Nelson, Hank Cochran, and Roger Miller whenever they asked. She also was famous for her hatpin, which she used to control anyone who got out of hand in her club. Tootsie Bess was a true patroness of the arts, and she's still missed in Nashville.

6. Radio stations WSM in Nashville and WLS in Chicago were the sponsors of the two most famous radio barn dance shows in history—the "Grand Old Opry" and the "National Barn Dance," respectively. Each of these stations was owned by a large business. WSM, which stands for "We Shelter Millions," is owned by the Nashville Casualty and Life Insurance Company, and for years, the company depended on the Opry to generate good will among the predominantly rural audience it solicited for business. WLS, which stands for "World's Largest Store," was owned by the Sears Roebuck company. Like WSM, Sears's sponsorship of a barn dance show was intended to generate consumer confidence in the business which sponsored it.

7. The Wabash Cannon Ball, subject of a song of the same name popularized by Roy Acuff, was a real train. In *Sing Your Heart Out, Country Boy,* author Dorothy Horstman says that the earliest mention of a train by that name occurred in 1885, when the now defunct Wabash Railroad used the name for its Chicago to Kansas City run. Although there was a version of the song "Wabash Cannon Ball" as early as 1905, Roy Acuff's recordings, made in 1937 and 1947, are the most popular

Buddy Emmons with his steel guitar.

renditions. The Cannon Ball is the most popular train in country music with the exception of the Orange Blossom Special, which ran from Miami, Florida, to New York City, and is said to have been the most powerful train in the world at the time it was running.

8. Luke the Drifter was the musical alter ego of Hank Williams. "Luke" usually recorded gospel and serious songs, while Hank made the more honky tonk records. Several Luke the Drifter songs are available on Hank Williams' reissue records.

9. The movie *Coal Miner's Daughter*, which starred Sissy Spacek and Tommy Lee Jones as Loretta and Mooney Lynn, was taken from Loretta's autobiography of the same name, and is substantially true, although some of the more painful parts of Loretta Lynn's life after she became a star have been glossed over. Loretta's friendship with the late Patsy Cline is partly fictionalized, because Loretta never toured with Cline in real life as she is shown doing in the film.

Other parts of the film are more true than people might suspect. The touring bus used toward the end of the film, for example, is Loretta's real bus, and is driven, on- and off-film, by her driver, Jim Webb. "Her" band is the same as the one Loretta uses in real life, and the antebellum mansion shown in the film is where she actually lives. The Washington state house, shown at the beginning of the movie, is really an old abandoned house on Loretta's ranch in Hurricane Mills.

10. The first country musicians used unamplified string instruments, and many traditionalists, especially in bluegrass bands, still do. It's probable that country musicians began to use electrically amplified guitar in the late thirties and early forties, when the noise of a crowded dance hall or a smokey honky tonk made the unamplified instrument difficult to hear. Leon McAuliffe, of Bob Wills and his Texas Playboys, was one of the first to use an amplified steel guitar, but the real pioneer in the field is said to have been Ernest Tubb, who ordered that an electrically amplified guitar be used on a 1941 recording of his because jukebox owners had complained to Tubb that his music couldn't be heard in the honky tonks. Tubb used electrically amplified instruments in his bands ever after. Rockabilly musicians also had a great influence on country guitar players, and the electric guitar was commonly used after 1956, even though some diehards felt that electrical amplification wasn't "pure."

EIGHTY
ESSENTIAL ALBUMS
FOR A COUNTRY MUSIC
RECORD COLLECTION

If I were asked to build a collection of country music records, taking into consideration the historical scope of the music, its varied styles, and, equally important, music which the listener will probably like and understand, I'd insist the following albums form the basis of the collection.

Every artist who has any real historical importance is at least represented,

Jerry Lee Lewis is presented with a unique memento of his single "I Can Still Hear the Music in the Restroom."

as are a few musicians who may not be historically important at all but who have made at least one record that distinguishes itself by the quality of the writing, the singing, or its ideas. On the other hand, some recordings which are usually mentioned in lists such as this one are omitted. I don't think it's really necessary to have the Library of Congress' recordings of Anglo-American ballads in order to understand country music. In fact, the sheer tedium of this kind of compilation

may put the average listener off the subject for good. In addition, I don't think it's necessary to include recordings of every person who made a record between 1920 and 1930 just because the recordings are old and there's a reissue available. Finally, I've omitted venerated folksingers like Woody Guthrie and Pete Seeger, because I don't think most urban folksingers have much to do with the creation of country music. You can bet that Hank Williams didn't listen to Woody Guthrie as a youngster, and I know for a fact that Loretta Lynn has never heard of Pete Seeger.

Instead, I have tried to accommodate both history and entertainment. The most famous country musicians are famous and influential because they were first entertaining. People liked them, and what's the use of having a record collection one can't enjoy? Therefore, I have not listed a single album on the basis that it's "good for you," even though it may bore you to tears.

Many of these records may be difficult to find: some are out of print, some are imports. To that, I can only say, "Try," because I guarantee they're worth the effort. I have all the records on this list, and I probably found more of them at K-Marts and garage sales than at record stores—the search is half the fun of making a collection anyhow.

Finally, I apologize if I've left out something you think is absolutely indispensable—but after all, it's my list.

ROY ACUFF

Greatest Hits, Vols. 1 and 2 (Elektra 9E-302, 9E-303): Today, Roy Acuff sounds dated—even if he does do a cover version of John Denver's "Thank God I'm A Country Boy" here—but when Acuff joined the Opry in the thirties, he amazed audiences and revolutionized country solo vocal style with his emotional, exhortative, gospel-flavored sound. Here you'll find his masterworks—"The Great Speckled Bird," "Wreck on the Highway," and "Wabash Cannon Ball"—as well as many of his lesser-known songs. And remember: this is the King Of Country Music singing, friends.

ASLEEP AT THE WHEEL

Comin' Right at Ya (United Artists UA-LA038F): This young swing band, whose membership varied from four to eleven members during its career—is single-handedly responsible for the revival of interest in western

swing that occurred during the seventies. Of the several albums the Wheel recorded, this is a personal favorite.

CHET ATKINS

The Night Atlanta Burned (RCA APL1-1233): Here, the best living country guitarist participates in a largely successful attempt to create a country music string quartet, with arrangements based on a mandolin orchestra score that was discovered in an instrument case dating from the Civil War. Atkins' virtuosity and intelligence are better displayed here than on any of his other work.

Guitar Monsters (with Les Paul RCA APL1-2786): Two great American pickers trade licks and jokes on this collaboration. That description sounds lightweight, but you won't think so when you hear how effortlessly Atkins and Paul handle the most complicated guitar runs.

GENE AUTRY

All American Cowboy/South of the Border (Republic IRDA-R-6011): America's favorite singing cowboy rides again, bringing you back to the days when the good guys wore white and the cowboy crooned a ballad at the drop of a ten-gallon hat. Although the sound of Autry's music is much more akin to the popular ballads of the forties, he began his career as a Jimmie Rodgers sound-alike, and his embodiment of the cowboy image helped change the country hero from an ignorant hillbilly to a knight in shining sequins.

BOBBY BARE

This Is Bobby Bare (VPS-6090): A two-record set of Bare's early sixties hits, including "Detroit City" and "500 Miles."

As Is (Columbia FC-37157): After going through *Down and Dirty* and *Drunk and Crazy* periods, Bare returned with this set of fine songs, which might better be called *Losin' and Leavin'*.

Clockwise from left:
Roy Acuff, "the King of Country Music"; an Opry touring group from the forties; Asleep at the Wheel tunes up; Bobby Bare.

THE BLUE SKY BOYS
(Bill and Earl Bolick)

The Blue Sky Boys (RCA Bluebird AXM2-5525): A proto-bluegrass duo, the Bolick Brothers probably had a great influence on Bill Monroe, but they're enjoyable even without historical rationalizations.

JOHNNY BUSH

Whiskey River/There Stands the Glass (RCA LSP-4817): An early fellow-traveler of Willie Nelson, Bush sings about the honky tonk life from years of experience. It shows.

THE CARTER FAMILY

The Original Carter Family, 1927–34, 1941 (RCA RA-5641-SO): Were I allowed to have only one country music record album, this ten-record set would probably be it. The Carter Family's huge repertoire, its still-fresh instrumental style, and the subtle emotionality of its singing style make it the definitive country music band. Unfortunately, this set is available only from Japan, and it'll set you back at least a hundred dollars should you be able to order it. It's more than worth the effort.

'Mid the Green Fields of Virginia (RCA LPM-2772): This is the best Carter Family set available in America. It contains the classics, and it's a fine sample of their sound, but for me, it's not enough.

The Carter Family on Border Radio (JEMF 101): Radio transcriptions of the family's programs broadcast from XERA in Villa Acuna, Mexico, compiled by the John Edwards Memorial Foundation in Los Angeles. This record not only helps the TV generation understand what these shows sounded like, but gives a pretty fair representation of the family's later work.

JOHNNY CASH

Original Golden Hits (Sun 100, 101, 127): These albums, available from the new Sun Records in Nashville, sum up Cash's rockabilly days nicely. They also include all his most famous songs, with the exception of "A Boy Named Sue."

Johnny Cash at Folsom Prison (Columbia CS9639): This live recording made Johnny Cash a national figure again in 1969, and the prison ambience makes the work a cultural artifact as well as a more than usually exciting live album.

ROSANNE CASH

Seven-Year Ache (Columbia JC36965): Rosanne may well be as talented as her daddy. This record, which stems from the California singer/songwriter school of country music, shows a feisty lady, a fine singer, and a promising writer.

PATSY CLINE

The Patsy Cline Story (MCA MCA2-4038): Patsy Cline, the best female song stylist ever to work with country music, was widely ignored after her death in a plane crash in 1963. Her friend Loretta Lynn helped to revive interest in Cline by recording an album of her songs, and by making the Cline role an important part of Lynn's movie biography, *Coal Miner's Daughter*. This set is a good summary of Cline's work.

BOB DYLAN

Nashville Skyline (Columbia KCS-9825): This recording helped greatly to make Nashville a legitimate place for "hip" people to work in 1969. Dylan used all Nashville session men on the album (including Charlie Daniels), and his duet with Johnny Cash—"Girl from the North Country"—is a classic, if for no other reason than that Dylan and Cash have the two most peculiar singing voices in America. The record also includes "Lay, Lady, Lay."

JOE ELY

Honky Tonk Masquerade (MCA MCA-2333): Joe Ely is from Lubbock, Texas, and is the best current exemplar of the sound of the

Joe Ely: the Lubbock sound.

KINKY FRIEDMAN

Sold American (Vanguard VSD-79333):
Kinky Friedman and his Texas Jewboys
were the most talented and most outrageous
act to emerge from the early outlaw country
scene. This album, simultaneously touching
and shocking, is a classic document of Jewish
country consciousness (an extremely short-
lived phenomenon), and of Kinky's extraordinary humor. Recommended by Willie and Waylon.

LEFTY FRIZZELL

The Legendary Lefty Frizzell (ABC ABCX-
799): Lefty Frizzell, born William Orville Frizzell in Corsicana, Texas, in 1928, is one of
country music's greatest singer-songwriters.
Although he was extremely popular in his
own right, especially during the 1950s when
he placed four songs in *Billboard*'s top ten
simultaneously, he is also important as *the*
major influence on four of country's best
male singers—Buck Owens, George Jones,
Willie Nelson, and Merle Haggard. In view of
this fact, it's hard to see why there aren't
more Lefty Frizzell records around. This album, recorded before Lefty's premature

region that produced Buddy Holly. This is an
early album, displaying Ely's songwriting abil-
ities and emotive country voice to its best advantage. His current work draws from rockabilly,
and he's become a hero of New Wave British
rock and rollers.

LESTER FLATT AND EARL SCRUGGS

Flatt and Scruggs At Carnegie Hall (Columbia CS-8845): Flatt and Scruggs, alumni
of Bill Monroe's Bluegrass Boys, made bluegrass music all the rage on college campuses
in the late sixties by playing for nonbluegrass
audiences such as this one. The music is bluegrass at its most accessible.

*Earl Scruggs' banjo helped repopularize
bluegrass in the late sixties.*

death of a stroke at the age of 47 in 1975, is, at best, a compromise. Still you'll hear several of Lefty's more famous songs, including "I Never Go Around Mirrors" and "I Can't Get Over You to Save My Life."

If you can possibly turn up a record with classics like "If You've Got the Money, I've Got the Time," or "Mom and Dad's Waltz," buy it instead of this record.

Lefty Frizzell (Columbia FC37466): Another compromise record, this reissue of some of Lefty's work in the early 1950s shows his vocal style still developing. I like it, even though it really falls into the "supplementary" rather than "essential" category.

JOHNNY GIMBLE

Texas Dance Party (Columbia KC-34284): Johnny Gimble is famous as Nashville's most popular session fiddle player. Before he played sessions, however, he played dances in Texas like this one, recorded live in 1975. Texas dance music, which is a little country, a little bluesy, a little Mexican, and a little German, is a distant subgenre of country music. Here it's played by the master.

MERLE HAGGARD

Songs I'll Always Sing (Capitol SABB-11531): Merle and his crack band, the Strangers, do Merle's classics. Haggard is arguably the best working songwriter in the business, and his style is unique. A good country music collection should contain as many Haggard albums as possible but this one will serve well for starters.

TOM T. HALL

Greatest Hits (Mercury SR-61369): Tom T. Hall's reputation as a songwriter is overrated. This album contains his best work, which is very good, but which was followed with junk like "I Like Beer" and "I Love . . . Little Baby Ducks." Still, one can't ignore "The Year Clayton Delaney Died" or "Homecoming."

Johnny Gimble and his good-time fiddle.

EMMYLOU HARRIS

Roses in the Snow (Warner Bros. BSK 3422): Just when I thought there'd never be another great girl singer, along came Emmylou Harris to show everyone how to do it. This album features bluegrass music and a wonderful band, along with classics that would have been lost had Emmylou not found them.

Blue Kentucky Girl (Warner Bros. BSK-3318): This record has Emmylou singing "hard" country—actually just old country. No one does a better interpretation of Louvin Brothers' songs in particular, and there are breathtaking versions of "Hickory Wind" and "Sorrow in the Wind."

BUDDY HOLLY

20 Golden Greats (MCA MCA-3040): Buddy Holly is remembered as a rock and roll idol, but when he began his career, such definitions were more limited: there was black music

and white music. If a Southern white boy didn't sound like Bing Crosby, he was classified as a hillbilly and packed off to Nashville to record, which is what happened to Buddy Holly. In fact, Holly's music was a mixture of Southern white and Southern black influences, and country audiences understood this music long before the rest of the nation did. That's why it's called rockabilly.

As is the case with the Carter Family, Buddy Holly's work is better represented abroad than in America. This is the best available American collection, and includes "Not Fade Away," "Peggy Sue," and the rest of Holly's most famous recordings.

A Rock and Roll Collection (Decca DXSE7-207): This is a more complete collection than the preceding one. It was once available as an American release, but is very difficult to find now, unless you obtain the British version, entitled *Legend.*

The Nashville Sessions (MCA-Coral CDLM-8038): This recording of the sessions Holly did in Nashville in 1956 is the one Holly record to own. It's now available as an import from England, and was once issued by Vocalion in the U.S. as *The Great Buddy Holly.* Produced by Owen Bradley, the mentor of Kitty Wells, Patsy Cline, and Loretta Lynn, it's the best example I've ever heard of the spooky quality that the best early rockabilly music possessed. There's a great version of "Rock Around with Ollie Vee."

WAYLON JENNINGS

Lonesome, On'ry and Mean (RCA LSP-4854): As with Merle Haggard, I'd advise you to have as many Waylon Jennings records as possible in your collection, but this one is a must. It was made when the outlaws were first feeling their oats, and there's a spirit in the songs that is often lacking in Jennings' later work.

Honky Tonk Heroes (RCA APL1-0240):

Emmylou Harris made the term "girl singer" respectable again.

The other absolute necessity in a Waylon collection, this record, which contains ten songs written by the brilliant Billy Joe Shaver, defines the modern country music hero, who just may be Waylon Jennings himself.

GEORGE JONES

George Jones (United Artists UXS-85): If you bought every record that George Jones—the world's greatest country singer—ever made, you'd have about two hundred albums. I wouldn't mind this myself, but for those who need to be convinced, this is a pretty fair collection of greatest hits.

All-Time Greatest Hits, Volume One (Epic KE-34692): Another collection—these rere-corded—of Jones classics, including "The Race Is On," "Why, Baby, Why?," and "Window Up Above." I can't see that recutting these songs has much diminished the quality as opposed to the originals, but purists may not agree.

The Battle (Epic KE-34034): Besides having the best cover I've ever seen on a country record, Jones's account of the domestic battlefield is, like so much of his work, half funny and half tragic. I'd love it if only for the title song.

The Grand Tour (Epic KE33083): The title song is *the* classic divorce song. Forget "D-I-V-O-R-C-E." If this song, sung the way George sings it, doesn't tear your heart out, you haven't got one.

I Am What I Am (Epic JE-36586): George's famous 1980 "comeback" album, for which he won his first CMA Award for best male singer. This record contains an unusual quantity—for a Jones album—of well-written songs, including "He Stopped Loving Her Today."

GEORGE JONES AND TAMMY WYNETTE

Greatest Hits (Epic KE-34716): Listen to this from the classic duet team, and you'll under-stand why so many of us wish George and Tammy were still married. This record contains my two favorite Jones and Wynette songs: "(We're Not) The Jet Set" and "Golden Ring."

KRIS KRISTOFFERSON

Me and Bobby McGee (Monument ZQ-31909): Although Kristofferson has written dozens of good songs, this record contains the songs that made the country music community recognize that the man they'd thought was a Commie hippie was, under all the hair, one of them. Kris made Nashville safe for people under 30 with this record.

JERRY LEE LEWIS

Original Golden Hits, Vols. 1–3 (Sun 102, 103, 128): This compilation encompasses the main body of the Killer's Sun recordings, from the revolutionary "Whole Lotta Shakin' Goin' On" to the arrogant "Great Balls of Fire." Just about any Jerry Lee Lewis album is a wonderful thing to own, but begin with these and work yourself out to the limits.

THE LOUVIN BROTHERS

Tragic Songs of Life (Capitol T-769): Without Ira and Charlie Louvin's painfully beautiful harmonies and equally gorgeous songs, there would have been no Everly Brothers, no Gram Parsons, no Emmylou Harris, and nobody for Johnny Cash to wish he could be when he grew up. The fact that the Louvins are relatively unknown is a crime, and should be rectified.

LORETTA LYNN

Greatest Hits, Vols. 1 and 2 (MCA-1: MCA-420): Loretta Lynn is the best writer and singer of songs about women who's ever lived.

George Jones, "the World's Greatest Country Singer." Inset: Kris Kristofferson, once a janitor, now a matinee idol.

George D. Hay with Uncle Dave Macon.

These records contain the ones she'll be most remembered for, and they must be in any collection, but I don't mind if you buy some of her other albums as well. You'll hear a unique mind at work.

UNCLE DAVE MACON

Early Recordings, 1925–1935 (County County-521): As you know, Uncle Dave Macon was the most popular of the Opry's early stars, but you needn't think of him as a quaint old fossil. Uncle Dave was pretty funny, and his

work holds up just fine today, while some of his contemporaries' music just sounds old.

BILL MONROE

Bean Blossom (MCA MCA 2-8002): It is difficult to find many recordings by the father of bluegrass music that were made during his early career. This two-record set, recorded during Monroe's annual bluegrass festival at Bean Blossom, Indiana, is representative of his work, which is generally impeccable, no matter which of his records you buy. You know nothing about bluegrass if you don't know the work of its inventor.

THE MONROE BROTHERS

Feast Here Tonight (RCA Bluebird AXM2-5510): Before he became "Daddy Bluegrass," Bill Monroe was merely part of the Monroe Brothers, a popular, but traditional, early string band, which offered Bill no chance to show off his mandolin and little opportunity to sing. Listening to this album will help you to understand the very big difference between old-fashioned country string music and the radical, rhythmic bluegrass that followed it. There are some good songs on this two-record set, especially Bill and Charlie Monroe's version of "He Will Set Your Fields on Fire."

WILLIE NELSON

And Then I Wrote (Liberty LST-7239): Now that Willie Nelson is being compared to people like Bing Crosby and Frank Sinatra, the fact that he's the author of some of the best country songs of the past two decades is too often forgotten. This album, made rather early in his career, will help to remind, as it contains both known songs and neglected classics, such as "This Is the Part Where I Cry."

Red-Headed Stranger (Columbia KC 33462): Unquestionably the best country concept album ever made, *Red-Headed Stranger*, the story of a man's fall from grace and painful return to it, is Willie Nelson's masterpiece. It can be analyzed in many ways: as a metaphor for the value system of the country music hero; as a religious parable; as a rejection of modern amorality; or, as Willie says he intended it, as a plot for a movie.

Phases and Stages (Atlantic SD-7291): This is Willie's almost-masterpiece. The record tells the story of a divorce, first from the man's point of view, then from the woman's. This ability to write from different perspectives is one of Nelson's special talents. While *Phases and Stages* is a distinguished work,

it lacks the universal qualities of *Red-Headed Stranger*, and so must be put in second place. The record contains one of Willie's most beautiful songs, "It's Not Supposed to Be That Way," with the famous admonition: "Be careful what you're dreamin', or soon your dreams will be dreamin' you."

Stardust (Columbia JC-35305): This record, with its easygoing renditions of old pop songs, made Willie Nelson a household name. My mama thinks it's real pretty. So will you.

MOLLY O'DAY

The Unforgettable Molly O'Day and the Cumberland Mountain Folks (Columbia/Harmony HL7299): This record will be difficult to find, but try your very best, because Molly O'Day is the best girl singer who ever lived, period. Had her career been longer—she recorded commercial country for only three years—she could have given Roy Acuff, Hank Williams, and maybe even George Jones a run for their money, for her music comes from the same traditions. As it is, she was the first person ever to record a Hank Williams song ("When God Comes to Gather His Jewels," included here); the first woman to lend deep, credible emotion to her music; and the first woman whose life had any real heroic qualities. The lady was a star.

BUCK OWENS

The Best of Buck Owens, Vols. 1, 2, 3, 4 (Capitol ST-2105, ST-2897; SKAO-145; ST-830): By working out of Bakersfield, California, rather than Nashville, Buck Owens and his "Bakersfield Sound" gave the country music establishment quite a shock during Buck's heyday in the early sixties. His work included more than a touch of rock and roll's rhythms, and his songs were often less than respectful by the standards of the times. Although Owens' career is in decline now, his contribution to modern country music is considerable. These albums illustrate why.

GRAM PARSONS

Sweetheart of the Rodeo, The Byrds (Columbia CS-9670): As a member of the Byrds, Gram Parsons was the major progenitor of country-rock music. He'd tried his ideas before when, as a member of the International Submarine Band, he made *Safe at Home. Sweetheart of the Rodeo* is the more famous of the two, however, and is considered to be the first country-rock album.

Gilded Palace of Sin, The Flying Burrito Brothers (A&M SP-4175): Parsons left the Byrds and joined this group, taking the name from an offshoot of the old International Submarine Band. A lesser-known but perhaps even better record than *Sweetheart,* Emmylou Harris says of it: "*Gilded Palace of Sin!* I mean, that's it!"

Grievous Angel (with Emmylou Harris, Warner Bros. MS-2171): The introduction of Emmylou Harris to the world and Gram Parsons' swan song (although he did make one more album, *GP* before his death). This record is absolutely beautiful.

DOLLY PARTON

Best of Dolly Parton (RCA LSP, 4449): This is not the *Best of Dolly Parton* that is usually recommended. There are two *Bests of,* and this one shows Dolly just before she entered her classic period, when her imagination was still a little morbid. The record includes "Down from Dover," the beautiful ballad about an unwed mother, which Dolly seldom performs anymore; and "Daddy, Come and Get Me," a *really* odd one, apparently about a ménage à trois.

Best of Dolly Parton (APL1-1117): This is the one usually recommended, and for good reason. No one, male or female, writes as well as Parton when she's at her best. Very few people sing as well as she does. This record contains her classics, especially the beautiful "Coat of Many Colors," and Parton was in the best of voices when the record was made.

DOLLY PARTON AND PORTER WAGONER

Porter and Dolly (RCA, AHL1-3700): Now that Dolly's a big movie star, people tend to forget that she started out as the girl singer on "The Porter Wagoner Show." She did, and Wagoner was no dummy for hiring her. Their voices mix well, and this album, released in 1981 as part of a professional settlement, is one of their best.

ELVIS PRESLEY

The Sun Sessions (RCA APM1-1675): For purposes of a country music collection, I think this record suffices. Those who collect Presley will collect him anyway; those who don't should have at least this album, which contains the most electrifying work of the Hillbilly Cat.

RAY PRICE

All-Time Greatest Hits (Columbia KE-31364): Ray Price was in Hank Williams' band, the Drifting Cowboys. Willie Nelson and Johnny Bush were in Ray's band, the Cherokee Cowboys. Price took the basic honky tonk genre, slicked it up a little for the Dallas sophisticates, and came up with a little corner of country music all his own.

JIM REEVES

He'll Have to Go (RCA LSP-2223): Reeves, inevitably described as "velvet-voiced," is probably country music's leading romantic hero. In fact, his style is so attractive to such a wide audience that RCA still issues an album of his songs every year, despite the fact that he was killed in a plane crash in 1964. Unless you're a diehard fan, this album will suffice, for historically Reeves will be remembered as country's first "easy listening" singer.

TEX RITTER

Tex Ritter, An American Legend (Capitol SKC-11241): Ole Tex was a Broadway actor,

The dream of Elvis Presley.

a star of singing cowboy movies, and an American institution as much as he was a country star, but he sure could sing those cowboy songs. Remember "High Noon"? He probably understood this kind of song better than most, but his singing talent was often eclipsed by the celebrity status of lesser singers such as Gene Autry and Roy Rogers.

JIMMIE RODGERS

This Is Jimmie Rodgers (RCA VPS-6091 [e]): Here we go again—Jimmie Rodgers, "the Father of Country Music," the man who influenced everybody, from Bob Wills to Roy Acuff, is best represented by a ten-record Japanese set. Since that set is hard to get,

most Americans will have to be satisfied with this two-record set, and with *Jimmie Rodgers: A Legendary Performer* (RCA CPL1-2504 [e]), both of which are available in the United States. Rodgers, who took blues, merged it with country, and became country music's patron saint, should be better represented in his own country.

BILLY JOE SHAVER

I'm Just an Ole Lump of Coal (But I'm Gonna Be a Diamond Someday) (Columbia FC-37078): Speaking of Ole Tex, I once heard him say that Billy Joe Shaver's "Willie the Wandering Gypsy and Me" was the best cowboy song

Tex Ritter, country's first Broadway star. Below: Billy Joe Shaver with Willie Nelson in the studio.

he'd heard in a coon's age. Billy Joe and his songs are about cowboys, but not the singing kind. A contemporary of Kris Kristofferson's (who was the first to record one of Billy Joe's songs), some people are of the opinion that Billy Joe writes better Kristofferson songs than Kris does. This album is an example of his recent work, and it's very impressive.

HANK SNOW

The Best Of Hank Snow, Vols. 1 and 2 (RCA LSP-3478, LSP-4798): Like Ernest Tubb, the Singing Ranger started out to emulate Jimmie Rodgers, but his robust voice was more suited to a modern style, and he's generally classified as an early honky tonk singer. His longevity alone—he was signed to RCA Canada in 1936—proves his quality and his lasting popularity.

SONS OF THE PIONEERS

Riders in the Sky (RCA ADL1-0336 [e]): If you're talking singing cowboys, you'd better smile when you mention the Sons of the Pioneers, who just about invented the singing cowboy. Most of the members weren't real cowboys, of course—lead singer and writer Bob Nolan was from Canada, and Leonard Slye (Roy Rogers) from Ohio—but this group recorded the best of the "movie cowboy" songs. They're responsible for "Cool Water," "Tumbling Tumbleweeds," "Ghost Riders in the Sky," and on and on. This music goes down right smooth.

THE STANLEY BROTHERS

Their Original Recordings (Melodeon MLPS-7322): Ralph and Carter Stanley are the ne plus ultra of bluegrass singing. Their high lonesome sounds will be too harsh for some listeners at first, but after you've grown accustomed to the style, you'll find that no one else, including Bill Monroe, sings with quite as much drive and emotion. Carter Stanley died several years ago, but Ralph carries on,

and if you like this record, several others are still available.

THE STATLER BROTHERS

Alive at the Johnny Mack Brown High School, Lester Roadhog Moran and his Cadillac Cowboys, (Mercury SR1-1708): This is the funniest country music record ever made. Ever. It is impossible to survive without it.

GARY STEWART

Out of Hand. (RCA APL1-0900): Some people argue that Moe Bandy is our best modern honky tonk singer, but my vote goes to Gary Stewart and especially to this album, which includes "Out of Hand," "Drinkin' Thing," and "She's Actin' Single." Stewart's erratic personality has stymied his career to date, but when he's good, Gary Stewart is one of modern country's music's greatest singers.

HANK THOMPSON

Back in the Swing of Things (ABC DOSD-2060): Hank Thompson and his Brazos Valley

Ralph Stanley: the high, lonesome sound.

Gary Stewart, heir apparent to George Jones.

Boys were a swing band in the tradition of Bob Wills and, during the fifties, were actually more popular than Wills himself. Perhaps this was because Thompson managed to inject a heavy dose of honky tonk music into the swing idiom, with songs like "I'm Not Mad, Just Hurt," "Squaws Along the Yukon," and "A Six Pack to Go." This record, which represents Hank's comeback after a dry period in the late sixties, isn't Thompson at his peak, but records from the earlier time are hard to find, and meanwhile, *Back in the Swing* is a fine substitute.

MERLE TRAVIS
Songs of the Coal Mines (Capitol T-1956): Merle Travis' guitar playing is so admired that both Chet Atkins and Doc Watson named

their sons after him. People forget, however, that Travis was one of our best songwriters, and this record, for which he composed and sings all the songs, is a classic. A Kentuckian, Travis knew the coal miner's life first-hand, and *Songs of the Coal Mines* documents that life about as well as it's ever been done.

The Best of Merle Travis (Capitol T-2662): This album contains Travis' more famous songs and also gives a fine picture of his widely imitated guitar style. Pay particular attention to "I Am a Pilgrim," "Dark as a Dungeon," and his biggest hit, "Sixteen Tons."

ERNEST TUBB
The Ernest Tubb Story (MCA MCA2-4040): Ernest Tubb began his career trying to sound like his hero, Jimmie Rodgers, and ended up

with a sound, a following, and an influence almost as pervasive as Rodgers' own. Tubb will be most remembered for his pioneering work in the honky tonk style, and here are honky tonk classics like "Slippin' Around," "Walkin' the Floor Over You," "Filipino Baby," and "I'll Get Along Somehow."

Ernest Tubb: The Legend and the Legacy (First Generation FGLP-0002): This album consists of Tubb singing his classics in duets with his friends. The list of friends tells how much Tubb is loved by the country music community. It includes Loretta Lynn, Willie Nelson, Waylon Jennings, George Jones, Charlie Rich, Merle Haggard, Johnny Cash, and Marty Robbins.

Hank Thompson.

VARIOUS ARTISTS

Will the Circle Be Unbroken? (United Artists UAS9801): This three-record set, made in 1971 under the aegis of the Nitty Gritty Dirt Band, made country music history in several ways. First, by getting "institutions" like Roy Acuff, Mother Maybelle Carter, and Merle Travis to agree to record with a "long-haired" band, it erased the separation between older country musicians and younger, "hip" players. Second, the recording sessions, which brought so many famous pickers together, was an event in itself. Finally, this record brought classic country music to the attention of young Americans and helped revive the popularity of both the performers and their work. Just about every cut here is extraordinary.

Stars of the Grand Ole Opry, 1926–1974 (RCA CPL2-0466): This two-record set was issued just as the Opry moved from the Ryman Auditorium to the new house at Opryland, and it includes performances by everybody, from Uncle Dave Macon to Dolly Parton. It's a good document of the program's history and preserves much of the spirit of fun that characterizes the best Opry shows. If you get a mint copy, you'll also get the country equivalent of a piece of the True Cross—a bit of the backdrop from the Opry stage is included in each package.

DOC WATSON

Memories (United Artists UA-LA423-H2): Doc Watson, the blind North Carolina guitarist and singer, was first recognized in folk music circles as an "old-time" musician. His participation in the recording of *Will the Circle Be Unbroken?* brought him to the attention of the commercial country community, albeit belatedly. His easygoing style and mellow voice show that he's much more modern than he was given credit for, and his blues-influenced style is well documented in songs like "Miss the Mississippi and You," "Blues,

Stay Away from Me," and "In the Jailhouse Now."

KITTY WELLS

The Kitty Wells Story (Decca XSB-7174): Here's the Queen of Country Music in all her glory. Kitty Wells, who first came to national attention with the forthright "It Wasn't God Who Made Honky Tonk Angels," set the standard for girl singers ever after. Wells was known as the first female honky tonk singer, although in private life she abhors the behavior she sings so well about. Even today, any girl singer worth her salt better be at least as good as Miss Kitty, or she isn't going to amount to a thing.

HANK WILLIAMS

The Immortal Hank Williams (MGM MM9097/106): Hank Williams is the most important country music singer who ever lived. He wrote classic after classic, his style became the criterion for judging all who followed him, and his life became the myth that the country music hero has tried to live ever since Hank's death in 1953. This is the best collection of his work, and, predictably, it's available only from Japan.

24 of Hank Williams' Greatest Hits (MGM SE4755-2): Of the numerous Hank Williams records available in the United States, this is the best, especially for those who may be unfamiliar with Hank's work. Looking at the

Hank Williams with his Drifting Cowboys.

songs included—among them "Your Cheatin' Heart," "I'm So Lonesome I Could Cry," "Cold, Cold Heart," and "Lovesick Blues," one is struck by the fact that anyone could, in a career as brief as Hank's, make almost every song he recorded a standard forever after.

BOB WILLS

Bob Wills Anthology (Columbia KG-32416): On these records, you will find the definition of western swing. Compiled from recordings made during the heyday of Bob Wills and his Texas Playboys in the forties, "the King of Western Swing" simply shows everyone else how to do it. From the lilting simplicity of a song like "New San Antonio Rose," to the jazzy "Big Beaver," to the virtuoso "Steel Guitar Rag," with its "Take it away, Leon!," Wills shows his mastery of many styles and his genius at synthesizing them into one so fresh and new.

For the Last Time (United Artists UA-LA216-J2): This four-record set is often recommended without informing the reader that the recordings were made after Wills had the devastating stroke that left him hardly able to function. Thus this record should be approached as an historical document—which it is, reuniting the Texas Playboys and

Wills's many admirers—rather than as a true reflection of his music at its best.

TAMMY WYNETTE

Tammy Wynette's Greatest Hits (Epic BN-26486): Add this record to the "greatest hits" collections of Dolly Parton and Loretta Lynn, and you will have examples of the work of the three most extraordinary women in country music, not to mention what will be considered to be two all-time classics—Tammy singing "Stand By Your Man" and "D-I-V-O-R-C-E." Tammy's style is a bit more modern than that of Loretta or Dolly, more sophisticated than the former and more stylized than the latter. This is a very classy record.

STEVE YOUNG

Seven Bridges Road (Blue Canyon BCS505): Like Gary Stewart, Steve Young's excellence as a singer and a songwriter has gone unrecognized by the public. This is Young's best album so far and includes his best work: the title song, "Montgomery in the Rain," "The White Trash Song," and "I Just Can't Seem to Hold Myself in Line." These songs are especially noteworthy for their exploration of the Southern American mind and ethic.

THE CMA AWARDS

The Country Music Association Awards, presented each year during the "Disc Jockey Convention" in October, are the country music equivalent of the Grammys. The awards program was begun in 1967 and is televised nationally from the stage of the new Opry House in Nashville. The winners are determined by a three-stage process. In the first round of voting, the five thousand members of the Country Music Association (made up of artists, disc jockeys, industry employees, and journalists) list their individual choices for prizes in each of ten categories. On the second ballot, voters make five choices in each category from a list that includes the names of everyone who received at least five votes on the first ballot. On the third ballot, which determines the ultimate winner, members vote for one person out of five, with the nominees being drawn from the top five choices from the second ballot.

The CMA Awards have often caused controversy among fans and the artists themselves. The fans howled in 1974, for example, when Australian pop singer Olivia Newton-John won the CMA's "Female Vocalist of the Year." Newton-John, said the fans—and some entertainers—was not "country." That dust-up led to the founding of a short-lived organization called ACE (Association of Country Entertainers), which was supposed to help keep country "country." There was a lot of heated talk for a while, but eventually the group broke up, when founding members such as Dolly Parton went to Hollywood and became movie stars.

Entertainers like Merle Haggard feel that the CMA Awards are too concerned with the mistaken idea of dignity and decorum. "[Country music] was built with Johnny Cash and Porter Wagoner and Marty Robbins and Hank Williams and Charley Pride and Merle Haggard and Buck Owens," Haggard told interviewer John Grissum. "These were the people who built country music. But when they have a goddamn award show they call on Tennessee Ernie Ford . . . Dale Evans, Roy Rogers, Champion . . . I just don't agree. I don't believe their theory is a winner. I believe their theory is a loser. And I think that their success would come quicker through country music being represented in the right manner."

The year after he made this statement, Merle Haggard was voted the CMA's Entertainer of the Year. The criteria for this highest of honors state that the award is "for the act displaying the greatest competence in all aspects of the entertainment field. Voter should give consideration not only to recorded performance, but also to in-person performance, staging, public acceptance, attitude, leadership, and overall contribution to the Country Music image."

That year, 1970, also happened to be the year that Haggard had a hit record with the hippie-baiting "Okie From Muskogee," a song that did not necessarily reflect Haggard's personal beliefs. One cannot help but wonder if Merle won the award for his own work or only because of the success of his song, even though the song did have a definite "attitude" and made a rather questionable "contribution to the Country Music image." Those who charge that the CMA Awards are too commercial have a point. George Jones, who's almost universally hailed as "the World's Greatest Country Singer," has been nominated for a CMA Award only ten times in his twenty-five-year career, and eight of those nominations were for "Vocal Duo of the Year" with ex-wife Tammy Wynette. The World's Greatest Country Singer finally won the CMA's "Male Vocalist of the Year" in 1980.

Finally, the CMA Awards have been criticized for showing a definite bias toward Nashville-based entertainers. This, too, is true, and it's one of the reasons that the Los Angeles-based Academy of Country Music was founded in 1964. Though the ACM Awards don't have the cachet of the CMA's, they do serve to recognize the too often overlooked West Coast country entertainer. An illustration of this is the fact that the CMA finally elected Bob Wills to the Country Music Hall of Fame

in 1968, seven years after the Hall of Fame was organized. Eddy Arnold beat Wills into the Hall of Fame by two years.

Despite these criticisms, Nashville is generally recognized as the power center of country music, and the CMA Awards usually get around to recognizing the best performers even though it may be later rather than sooner.

The CMA Award categories are: Entertainer of the Year; Single of the Year; Album of the Year; Song of the Year (a writer's award based on nominations of the membership as well as the top five songs as tabulated by the trade magazines *Billboard, Cash Box, The Gavin Report, Radio and Records,* and *Record World*); Female Vocalist of the Year; Male Vocalist of the Year; Vocal Group of the Year; Vocal Duo of the Year; Instrumental Group or Band of the Year; and Instrumentalist of the Year. In addition, the CMA's Board of Directors makes nominations in two categories: for membership in the Country Music Hall of Fame, and for the Horizon Award, recognizing new talent, instituted in 1981 and voted upon on the second and third ballots.

Winners in each category since 1967 are:

CATEGORY 1:
Entertainer of the Year
1967	Eddy Arnold
1968	Glen Campbell
1969	Johnny Cash
1970	Merle Haggard
1971	Charley Pride
1972	Loretta Lynn
1973	Roy Clark
1974	Charlie Rich
1975	John Denver
1976	Mel Tillis
1977	Ronnie Milsap
1978	Dolly Parton
1979	Willie Nelson
1980	Barbara Mandrell
1981	Barbara Mandrell

CATEGORY 2:

Single of the Year

1967   "There Goes My Everything" / Jack Greene / Decca
1968   "Harper Valley PTA" / Jeannie C. Riley / Plantation
1969   "A Boy Named Sue" / Johnny Cash / Columbia
1970   "Okie from Muskogee" / Merle Haggard / Capitol
1971   "Help Me Make It Through the Night" / Sammi Smith / Mega
1972   "The Happiest Girl in the Whole USA" / Donna Fargo / Dot
1973   "Behind Closed Doors" / Charlie Rich / Epic
1974   "Country Bumpkin" / Cal Smith / MCA
1975   "Before the Next Teardrop Falls" / Freddy Fender / ABC-Dot
1976   "Good-Hearted Woman" / Waylon Jennings & Willie Nelson / RCA
1977   "Lucille" / Kenny Rogers / UA
1978   "Heaven's Just a Sin Away" / The Kendalls / Ovation
1979   "The Devil Went Down to Georgia" / Charlie Daniels Band / Epic
1980   "He Stopped Loving Her Today" / George Jones / Epic
1981   "Elvira" / The Oak Ridge Boys / MCA

CATEGORY 3:

Album of the Year

1967   *There Goes My Everything* / Jack Greene / Decca
1968   *Johnny Cash at Folsom Prison* / Johnny Cash / Columbia
1969   *Johnny Cash at San Quentin Prison* / Johnny Cash / Columbia
1970   *Okie From Muskogee* / Merle Haggard / Capitol
1971   *I Won't Mention It Again* / Ray Price / Columbia

1972   *Let Me Tell You About a Song* / Merle Haggard / Capitol
1973   *Behind Closed Doors* / Charlie Rich / Epic
1974   *A Very Special Love Song* / Charlie Rich / Epic
1975   *A Legend in My Time* / Ronnie Milsap / RCA
1976   *Wanted: The Outlaws* / Waylon Jennings, Willie Nelson, Tompall Glaser, Jessi Colter / RCA
1977   *Ronnie Milsap Live* / Ronnie Milsap / RCA
1978   *It Was Almost Like a Song* / Ronnie Milsap / RCA
1979   *The Gambler* / Kenny Rogers / UA
1980   *Coal Miner's Daughter (Original Motion Picture Soundtrack)* / MCA
1981   *I Believe in You* / Don Williams / MCA

CATEGORY 4:

Song of the Year

1967   "There Goes My Everything" / Dallas Frazier
1968   "Honey" / Bobby Russell
1969   "Carroll County Accident" / Bob Ferguson
1970   "Sunday Morning Coming Down" / Kris Kristofferson
1971   "Easy Loving" / Freddie Hart
1972   "Easy Loving" / Freddie Hart
1973   "Behind Closed Doors" / Kenny O'Dell
1974   "Country Bumpkin" / Don Wayne
1975   "Back Home Again" / John Denver
1976   "Rhinestone Cowboy" / Larry Weiss
1977   "Lucille" / Roger Bowling & Hal Bynum
1978   "Don't It Make My Brown Eyes Blue" / Richard Leigh
1979   "The Gambler" / Don Schlitz / Writers Night Music
1980   "He Stopped Loving Her Today" / Bobby Braddock and Curly Putnam / Tree International

Jerry Lee Lewis at the 1981 CMA Awards show. Below: Charlie Daniels without his hat! Charlie won Instrumentalist of the Year in 1979.

1981 "He Stopped Loving Her Today" /
      Bobby Braddock and Curly Putnam /
      Tree International

CATEGORY 5:

Female Vocalist of the Year

1967 Loretta Lynn
1968 Tammy Wynette
1969 Tammy Wynette
1970 Tammy Wynette
1971 Lynn Anderson
1972 Loretta Lynn
1973 Loretta Lynn
1974 Olivia Newton-John
1975 Dolly Parton
1976 Dolly Parton
1977 Crystal Gayle
1978 Crystal Gayle
1979 Barbara Mandrell
1980 Emmylou Harris
1981 Barbara Mandrell

CATEGORY 6:

Male Vocalist of the Year

1967 Jack Greene
1968 Glen Campbell
1969 Johnny Cash
1970 Merle Haggard
1971 Charley Pride
1972 Charley Pride
1973 Charlie Rich
1974 Ronnie Milsap
1975 Waylon Jennings
1976 Ronnie Milsap
1977 Ronnie Milsap
1978 Don Williams
1979 Kenny Rogers
1980 George Jones
1981 George Jones

CATEGORY 7:

Vocal Group of the Year

1967 The Stoneman Family
1968 Porter Wagoner and Dolly Parton
1969 Johnny Cash and June Carter
1970 The Glaser Brothers
1971 The Osborne Brothers
1972 The Statler Brothers
1973 The Statler Brothers
1974 The Statler Brothers
1975 The Statler Brothers
1976 The Statler Brothers
1977 The Statler Brothers
1978 The Oak Ridge Boys
1979 The Statler Brothers
1980 The Statler Brothers
1981 Alabama

CATEGORY 8:

Vocal Duo of the Year

(added in 1970)

1970 Porter Wagoner and Dolly Parton
1971 Porter Wagoner and Dolly Parton
1972 Conway Twitty and Loretta Lynn
1973 Conway Twitty and Loretta Lynn
1974 Conway Twitty and Loretta Lynn
1975 Conway Twitty and Loretta Lynn
1976 Waylon Jennings and Willie Nelson
1977 Jim Ed Brown and Helen Cornelius
1978 Kenny Rogers and Dottie West
1979 Kenny Rogers and Dottie West
1980 Moe Bandy and Joe Stampley
1981 David Frizzell and Shelly West

CATEGORY 9:

Instrumental Group or Band of the Year

1967 The Buckaroos
1968 The Buckaroos
1969 Danny Davis and the Nashville Brass
1970 Danny Davis and the Nashville Brass
1971 Danny Davis and the Nashville Brass
1972 Danny Davis and the Nashville Brass
1973 Danny Davis and the Nashville Brass
1974 Danny Davis and the Nashville Brass
1975 Roy Clark and Buck Trent
1976 Roy Clark and Buck Trent
1977 The Original Texas Playboys
1978 The Oak Ridge Boys Band

1979   The Charlie Daniels Band
1980   The Charlie Daniels Band
1981   Alabama

CATEGORY 10:

Instrumentalist of the Year

1967   Chet Atkins
1968   Chet Atkins
1969   Chet Atkins
1970   Jerry Reed
1971   Jerry Reed
1972   Charlie McCoy
1973   Charlie McCoy
1974   Don Rich
1975   Johnny Gimble

1976   Hargus "Pig" Robbins
1977   Roy Clark
1978   Roy Clark
1979   Charlie Daniels
1980   Roy Clark
1981   Chet Atkins

CATEGORY 11:

Comedian of the Year

(discontinued in 1971)

1967   Don Bowman
1968   Ben Colder
1969   Archie Campbell
1970   Roy Clark

THE GRAMMY AWARDS

Remember Domenico Modugno? He won the first Grammy award for *"Nel Blu Dipinto Di Blu (Volare)"* in 1958. The Grammy—named after the gramophone—is an industry-wide music awards program administered by the National Academy of Recording Arts and Sciences, or NARAS. Although the Grammys are best known as awards for popular recording artists, there have been one or more country music categories in the program since its beginning, and many country performers would rather win the Grammy than the CMA award, because of the former's national scope.

Grammy nominations and winners are determined by the votes of five thousand NARAS members, all of whom must have been involved in some aspect of the production of a record (e.g., as musician, producer, engineer, annotator, songwriter) in order to be eligible to vote. Since jazz, classical, rock, pop, and various ethnic categories are as heavily represented in the NARAS membership as is country, country music Grammys have historically tended to go to the song or singer who enjoyed the widest national popularity during the voting year.

For this reason, one performer or singer will occasionally "sweep" the Grammy awards, as did Roger Miller in 1964 and 1965 and Glen Campbell in 1967 and 1968. In addition, from time to time there seems to be some confusion over what is country music. In 1959, for example, the Kingston Trio won the country award for "Tom Dooley," which is, strictly speaking, a folk song, not a country song. In 1962 Burl Ives won the country award for "Funny Way of Laughin'," while Ray Charles won the rhythm and blues prize with the classic country song "I Can't Stop Loving You." In the early seventies, country awards usually went to pop performers like Olivia Newton-John and Anne Murray. Real country performers like Willie Nelson and George Jones didn't win their first solo Grammys until 1978 and 1980, respectively.

Still, a look at Grammy winners can be instructive, because one can see the ebb and flow of various styles, not to mention the ups and downs of various careers. And, lest you take these awards too seriously, it's interesting to note that Elvis Presley won only three Grammys, all for "sacred" or "inspirational" performances, and that the Beatles, as a group, won only four, two in 1964 and two in 1967.

Here's a list of country Grammy winners, and Grammys won by noncountry acts that may be of interest to the country fan. Note that the categories change from year to year.

1958

Best Country & Western Performance:
"Tom Dooley" / The Kingston Trio

1959

Best Country & Western Performance:
"The Battle of New Orleans" / Johnny Horton
Song of the Year:
"The Battle of New Orleans" / Jimmy Driftwood
Best Comedy Performance—Musical:
"The Battle of Kookamonga" / Homer and Jethro
Best Performance—Folk:
The Kingston Trio at Large / The Kingston Trio

1960

Best Country & Western Performance:
"El Paso" / Marty Robbins
Best Performance by a Pop Single Artist:
"Georgia On My Mind" / Ray Charles
Best Performance by a Chorus:
Songs of the Cowboy / The Norman Luboff Choir

1961

Best Country & Western Recording:
"Big Bad John" / Jimmy Dean

1962

Best Country & Western Recording:
"Funny Way of Laughin' " / Burl Ives
Best Rhythm & Blues Recording:
"I Can't Stop Loving You" / Ray Charles

1963

Best Country & Western Recording:
"Detroit City" / Bobby Bare

Best Rhythm & Blues Recording:
"Busted" / Ray Charles
Best Instrumental Arrangement:
"I Can't Stop Loving You" / Quincy Jones (arranger)

1964

Best Country & Western Single:
"Dang Me" / Roger Miller
Best Country & Western Album:
Dang Me / *Chug-a-Lug* / Roger Miller
Best Country & Western/Vocal Performance, Female:
"Here Comes My Baby" / Dottie West
Best Country & Western/Vocal Performance, Male:
"Dang Me" / Roger Miller
Best Country & Western Song:
"Dang Me" / Roger Miller
Best New Country & Western Artist of 1964:
Roger Miller

1965

Best Country & Western Single:
"King of the Road" Roger Miller
Best Country & Western Album:
The Return of Roger Miller / Roger Miller
Best Country & Western Vocal Performance, Female:
"Queen of the House" / Jody Miller
Best Country & Western Vocal Performance, Male:
"King of the Road" / Roger Miller
Best Country & Western Song:
"King of the Road" / Roger Miller
Best New Country & Western Artist:
The Statler Brothers
Best Contemporary (R&R) Single:
"King of the Road" / Roger Miller
Best Contemporary (R&R) Vocal Performance, Male:
"King of the Road" / Roger Miller
Best Contemporary (R&R) Performance, Group (Vocal or Instrumental):
"Flowers on the Wall" / The Statler Brothers

1966

Best Country & Western Recording:
Almost Persuaded / David Houston
Best Country & Western Vocal
Performance, Female:
"Don't Touch Me" / Jeannie Seely
Best Country & Western Vocal
Performance, Male:
"Almost Persuaded" / David Houston
Best Country & Western Song:
"Almost Persuaded" / Billy Sherrill and Glenn
Sutton
Best Sacred Recording (Musical):
Grand Ole Gospel / Porter Wagoner and the
Blackwood Brothers

Best Album Cover, Photography:
Confessions of a Broken Man / Porter
Wagoner / Les Leverette, photographer

1967

Best Country & Western Recording:
Gentle on My Mind / Glen Campbell
Best Country & Western Solo Vocal
Performance, Female:
"I Don't Wanna Play House" / Tammy
Wynette
Best Country & Western Solo Vocal
Performance, Male:
Gentle on My Mind / Glen Campbell

Best Country & Western Performance, Duet, Trio, or Group:
"Jackson" / Johnny Cash and June Carter
Best Country & Western Song:
"Gentle on My Mind" / Glen Campbell / John Hartford
Best Folk Performance:
"Gentle on My Mind" / John Hartford
Best Sacred Performance:
How Great Thou Art / Elvis Presley
Best Vocal Performance, Female (pop):
"Ode to Billie Joe" / Bobbie Gentry
Best Vocal Performance, Male (pop):
"By the Time I Get to Phoenix" / Glen Campbell

Opposite: *Elvis, here dancing with his girl at home in Memphis, won only three Grammy awards.* **Below:** *Bobby Bare won the Grammy in 1963 for "Detroit City."* **Right:** *Emmylou Harris won Grammys in 1976 and 1979 for* Elite Hotel *and* Blue Kentucky Girl, *respectively.*

Best New Artist:
Bobbie Gentry
Best Contemporary Female Solo Vocal Performance:
Ode to Billie Joe / Bobbie Gentry
Best Contemporary Male Solo Vocal Performance:
"By the Time I Get to Phoenix" / Glen Campbell
Best Album Notes:
Suburban Attitudes in Country Verse / John D. Loudermilk

1968
Best Country Vocal Performance, Female:
"Harper Valley PTA" / Jeannie C. Riley
Best Country Vocal Performance, Male:
"Folsom Prison Blues" / Johnny Cash
Best Country Performance, Duo or Group (Vocal or Instrumental):
"Foggy Mountain Breakdown" / Flatt and Scruggs
Best Country Song:
"Little Green Apples" / Bobby Russell
Album of the Year:
By the Time I Get to Phoenix / Glen Campbell
Song of the Year:
"Little Green Apples" / Bobby Russell
Best Engineered Recording:
Wichita Lineman / Glen Campbell / Joe Polito and Hugh Davies, Engineers
Best Album Notes:
Johnny Cash at Folsom Prison / Johnny Cash, annotator

1969
Best Country Vocal Performance, Female:
Stand By Your Man / Tammy Wynette
Best Country Vocal Performance, Male:
"A Boy Named Sue" / Johnny Cash
Best Country Performance, Duo or Group:
"MacArthur Park" / Waylon Jennings and the Kimberleys
Best Country Instrumental Performance:
The Nashville Brass Featuring Danny

Davis Play More Nashville Sounds / Danny Davis and the Nashville Brass
Best Country Song:
"A Boy Named Sue" / Shel Silverstein
Best Gospel Performance:
In Gospel Country / Porter Wagoner and the Blackwood Brothers
Song of the Year:
"Games People Play" / Joe South
Best Album Notes:
Nashville Skyline / Bob Dylan / Johnny Cash, annotator
Best Contemporary Song:
"Games People Play" / Joe South
Best Rhythm & Blues Instrumental Performance:
"Games People Play" / King Curtis

1970
Best Country Vocal Performance, Female:
"Rose Garden" / Lynn Anderson
Best Country Vocal Performance, Male:
"For the Good Times" / Ray Price
Best Country Performance, Duo or Group:
If I Were a Carpenter / Johnny Cash and June Carter
Best Country Instrumental Performance:
Me & Jerry / Chet Atkins and Jerry Reed
Best Country Song:
"My Woman, My Woman, My Wife" / Marty Robbins
Best Gospel Performance (Other than Soul Gospel):
Talk About The Good Times / The Oak Ridge Boys
Best Contemporary Vocal Performance, Male:
"Everything Is Beautiful" / Ray Stevens

1971
Best Country Vocal Performance, Female:
"Help Me Make It Through the Night" / Sammi Smith
Best Country Vocal Performance, Male:
"When You're Hot You're Hot" / Jerry Reed

Best Country Vocal Performance, Group:
"After the Fire Is Gone" / Conway Twitty and Loretta Lynn
Best Country Instrumental Performance:
"Snowbird" / Chet Atkins
Best Country Song:
"Help Me Make It Through the Night" / Kris Kristofferson
Best Gospel Performance (Other than Soul Gospel):
Let Me Live / Charley Pride

1972

Best Country Vocal Performance, Female:
"Happiest Girl in the Whole USA" / Donna Fargo
Best Country Vocal Performance, Male:
Charley Pride Sings Heart Songs / Charley Pride
Best Country Vocal Performance, Duo or Group:
"Class of '57" / The Statler Brothers
Best Country Instrumental Performance:
Charlie McCoy / The Real McCoy / Charlie McCoy
Best Country Song:
"Kiss an Angel Good Morning" / Ben Peters
Best Inspirational Performance:
He Touched Me / Elvis Presley
Best Album Notes:
Tom T. Hall's Greatest Hits / Tom T. Hall, annotator

1973

Best Country Vocal Performance, Female:
"Let Me Be There" / Olivia Newton-John
Best Country Vocal Performance, Male:
"Behind Closed Doors" / Charlie Rich
Best Country Vocal Performance, Duo or Group:
"From the Bottle to the Bottom" / Kris Kristofferson and Rita Coolidge
Best Country Song:
"Behind Closed Doors" / Kenny O'Dell
Best Ethnic or Traditional Recording:
Then And Now / Doc Watson

1974

Best Country Vocal Performance, Female:
Love Song / Anne Murray
Best Country Vocal Performance, Male:
"Please Don't Tell Me How the Story Ends" / Ronnie Milsap
Best Country Vocal Performance, Duo or Group:
"Fairytale" / The Pointer Sisters
Best Country Instrumental Performance:
The Atkins-Travis Traveling Show / Chet Atkins and Merle Travis
Best Country Song:
"A Very Special Love Song" / Norro Wilson and Billy Sherrill
Best Album Notes:
For The Last Time / Bob Wills and his Texas Playboys / Charles R. Townsend, annotator

1975

Best Country Vocal Performance, Female:
"I Can't Help It (If I'm Still in Love With You)" / Linda Ronstadt
Best Country Vocal Performance, Male:
"Blue Eyes Crying in the Rain" / Willie Nelson
Best Country Vocal Performance, Duo or Group:
"Lover Please" / Kris Kristofferson and Rita Coolidge
Best Country Instrumental Performance:
"The Entertainer" / Chet Atkins
Best Country Song:
"(Hey Won't You Play) Another Somebody Done Somebody Wrong Song" / Chips Moman and Larry Butler
Best Pop Vocal Performance, Duo, Group, or Chorus:
"Lyin' Eyes" / The Eagles

1976

Best Country Vocal Performance, Female:
Elite Hotel / Emmylou Harris
Best Country Vocal Performance, Male:
"(I'm a) Stand By My Woman Man" / Ronnie Milsap

Best Country Vocal Performance, Duo or Group:
"The End Is Not in Sight (The Cowboy Tune)" / The Amazing Rhythm Aces
Best Country Instrumental Performance:
Chester & Lester / Chet Atkins and Les Paul
Best Country Song:
"Broken Lady" / Larry Gatlin
Best Gospel Performance:
"Where the Soul Never Dies" / The Oak Ridge Boys
Best Ethnic or Traditional Recording:
Mark Twang / John Hartford

1977

Best Country Vocal Performance, Female:
"Don't It Make My Brown Eyes Blue" / Crystal Gayle
Best Country Vocal Performance, Male:
"Lucille" / Kenny Rogers
Best Country Vocal Performance, Duo or Group:
"Heaven's Just a Sin Away" / The Kendalls
Best Country Instrumental Performance:
Country Instrumentalist of the Year / Hargus "Pig" Robbins
Best Country Song:
"Don't It Make My Brown Eyes Blue" / Richard Leigh
Record of the Year:
Hotel California / The Eagles

1978

Best Country Vocal Performance, Female:
Here You Come Again / Dolly Parton
Best Country Vocal Performance, Male:
"Georgia on My Mind" / Willie Nelson
Best Country Vocal Performance, Duo or Group:
"Mamas, Don't Let Your Babies Grow Up to Be Cowboys" / Willie Nelson and Waylon Jennings
Best Country Instrumental Performance:
"One O'Clock Jump" / Asleep at the Wheel
Best Country Song:
"The Gambler" / Don Schlitz

1979

Best Country Vocal Performance, Female:
Blue Kentucky Girl / Emmylou Harris
Best Country Vocal Performance, Male:
"The Gambler" / Kenny Rogers
Best Country Vocal Performance, Duo or Group:
"The Devil Went Down to Georgia" / The Charlie Daniels Band
Best Country Instrumental Performance:
"Big Sandy/Leather Britches" / Doc and Merle Watson
Best Country Song:
"You Decorated My Life" / Bob Morrison and Debbie Hupp

1980

Best Country Vocal Performance, Female:
"Could I Have This Dance? / Anne Murray
Best Country Vocal Performance, Male:
"He Stopped Loving Her Today" / George Jones
Best Country Vocal Performance, Duo or Group:
"That Lovin' You Feelin' Again" / Emmylou Harris and Roy Orbison
Best Country Instrumental Performance:
"Orange Blossom Special/Hoedown" / Gilley's Urban Cowboy Band
Best Country Song:
"On the Road Again" / Willie Nelson

1981

Best Country Vocal Performance, Female:
"Nine to Five" / Dolly Parton
Best Country Vocal Performance, Male:
"(There's) No Gettin' Over Me" / Ronnie Milsap
Best Country Vocal Performance, Duo or Group:
"Elvira" / The Oak Ridge Boys
Best Country Instrumental Performance:
Country—After All These Years / Chet Atkins
Best Country Song:
"Nine to Five" / Dolly Parton

GOLD AND PLATINUM RECORDS

Newspaper and magazine articles about country musicians almost always mention how many gold and platinum records an artist has been awarded, but usually don't explain the criteria for the awards. Record companies used to give so-called "gold" awards to their best-selling artists, but the only ones that really count are those awarded by the Recording Industry Association of America, known as the RIAA, which began the practice in 1959.

The RIAA, a record manufacturers' trade group, certifies a record for gold or platinum status only after auditing the record company's sales records. From 1959 until 1976, gold records were awarded to singles or albums that earned a million dollars in manufacturer's sales. In 1976 the platinum award, signifying sales of one million copies, was instituted. During the same year standards for the gold award were changed, and gold records now go to any album that sells 500,000 or more copies, and to any single that sells at least a million copies. A platinum single must sell two million copies. The actual awards, by the way, are not made of real gold or plati num—they're only copies of the album dipped in gold or silver paint.

COUNTRY ARTISTS WHO'VE WON RIAA CERTIFIED GOLD AND PLATINUM RECORDS

1959

Ernie Ford / *Hymns* / Capitol

1961

Ernie Ford / *Spirituals* / *Capitol*
Jimmy Dean / *Big Bad John* / Columbia

1962

Ernie Ford / *Star Carol* / Capitol
Ernie Ford / *Nearer the Cross* / Capitol

1964

Johnny Horton / *Johnny Horton's Greatest Hits* / Columbia

1965

Johnny Cash / *Ring of Fire* / Columbia
Roger Miller / "King of the Road" / Smash
Roger Miller / *Return of Roger Miller* / Smash
Marty Robbins / *Gunfighter Ballads & Trail Songs* / Columbia

1966

Roger Miller / *Golden Hits* / Smash
Eddy Arnold / *My World* / RCA
Jim Reeves / *The Best of Jim Reeves* / RCA
Roger Miller / *Dang Me* / Smash
Johnny Horton / "Battle of New Orleans" / Columbia

1967

Johnny Cash / *I Walk the Line* / Columbia
Bobbie Gentry / "Ode to Billie Joe" / Capitol
Bobbie Gentry / *Ode to Billie Joe* / Capitol

1968

Jim Reeves / *Distant Drums* / RCA
Buck Owens / *Best Of Buck Owens* / Capitol
Eddy Arnold / *Best Of Eddy Arnold* / RCA
Jeannie C. Riley / "Harper Valley PTA" / Plantation
Glen Campbell / *By the Time I Get to Phoenix* / Capitol
Glen Campbell / *Gentle on My Mind* / Capitol
Johnny Cash / *Johnny Cash at Folsom Prison* / Columbia
Glen Campbell / *Wichita Lineman* / Capitol
Jeannie C. Riley / *Harper Valley PTA* / Plantation

1969

Glen Campbell / *Hey Little One* / Capitol
Glen Campbell / "Wichita Lineman" / Capitol
Glen Campbell & Bobbie Gentry / *Gentry/Campbell* / Capitol
Glen Campbell / *Galveston* / Capitol
Hank Williams / *Hank Williams Greatest Hits* / MGM
Hank Williams / *Your Cheatin' Heart* / MGM
Johnny Cash / *Johnny Cash's Greatest Hits* / Columbia
Johnny Cash / *Johnny Cash at San Quentin* / Columbia
Johnny Cash / "A Boy Named Sue" / Columbia
Glen Campbell / *Glen Campbell Live* / Capitol
Glen Campbell / "Galveston" / Capitol
Gene Autry / *Rudolph the Red-Nosed Reindeer* / Columbia

1970

Charley Pride / *The Best of Charley Pride* / RCA
Johnny Cash / *Hello, I'm Johnny Cash* / Columbia
Glen Campbell / *Try a Little Kindness* / Capitol
Loretta Lynn / *Don't Come Home A-Drinkin'* / Decca
Tammy Wynette / *Tammy's Greatest Hits* / Epic
Anne Murray / "Snowbird" / Capitol

1971

Lynn Anderson / "Rose Garden" / Columbia
Charley Pride / *Charley Pride's 10th Album* / RCA
Charley Pride / *Just Plain Charley* / RCA
Charley Pride / *Charley Pride In Person* / RCA
Ray Price / *For the Good Times* / Columbia
Merle Haggard / *The Fightin' Side of Me* / Capitol
Lynn Anderson / *Rose Garden* / Columbia
Jerry Reed / "Amos Moses" / RCA
Freddy Hart / "Easy Lovin' " / Capitol
Johnny Cash / *The World of Johnny Cash* / Columbia

1972

Loretta Lynn / *Loretta Lynn's Greatest Hits* / Decca
Charley Pride / *Charley Pride Sings Heart Songs* / RCA
Charley Pride / "Kiss an Angel Good Morning" / RCA
Glen Campbell / *Glen Campbell's Greatest Hits* / Capitol
Conway Twitty / *Hello Darlin'* / Decca
Donna Fargo / "Happiest Girl in the Whole USA" / Dot
Mac Davis / "Baby Don't Get Hooked on Me" / Columbia
Charley Pride / *Best of Charley Pride* / RCA

Freddy Hart / *Easy Lovin'* / Capitol
Merle Haggard / *Best of Merle Haggard* / Capitol

1973

Donna Fargo / *Happiest Girl in the Whole USA* / Dot
Kenny Rogers & 1st Edition / *Kenny Rogers & the 1st Edition Greatest Hits* / Warner/Reprise
Charley Pride / *The Sensational Charley Pride* / RCA
Charley Pride / *From Me to You* / RCA
Kris Kristofferson / "Why Me" / Monument
Kris Kristofferson / *The Silver Tongued Devil and I* / Monument
Charlie Rich / *Behind Closed Doors* / Epic
Kris Kristofferson / *Jesus Was a Capricorn* / Monument
Charlie Rich / "The Most Beautiful Girl" / Epic
Anne Murray / *Snowbird* / Capitol
Donna Fargo / "Funny Face" / Dot
Charlie Rich / "Behind Closed Doors" / Epic

1974

Jim Stafford / "Spiders and Snakes" / MGM
Charlie Rich / *Very Special Love Song* / Epic
Ray Stevens / "The Streak" / Barnaby
Merle Haggard / *The Best of Merle Haggard* / Capitol
Mac Davis / *Stop and Smell the Roses* / Columbia
Charlie Rich / *There Won't Be Anymore* / RCA
Billy Swan / "I Can Help" / Monument
Kris Kristofferson / *Me and Bobby McGee* / Monument

1975

Charley Pride / *Did You Think to Pray?* / RCA
Charley Pride / *(Country) Charley Pride* / RCA

Charlie Daniels Band / *Fire on the Mountain* / Kama Sutra
Freddy Fender / *Before the Next Teardrop Falls* / ABC/Dot
Glen Campbell / "Rhinestone Cowboy" / Capitol
C. W. McCall / "Convoy" / MGM

Glen Campbell / *Rhinestone Cowboy* / Capitol
Freddy Fender / "Before the Next Teardrop Falls" / ABC/Dot
Freddy Fender / "Wasted Days & Wasted Nights" / ABC/Dot

1976

C. W. McCall / *Black Bear Road* / MGM
Willie Nelson / *Red-Headed Stranger* /
Columbia
*Waylon, Willie, Tompall, Jessi / *The
Outlaws* / RCA
Conway Twitty / *You've Never Been This Far
Before/Baby's Gone* / MCA
Mac Davis / *All the Love in the World* /
Columbia
Glen Campbell / *The Christmas Feeling* /
Capitol
Jimmy Dean / "I.O.U." / GRT/Casino
Red Sovine / "Teddy Bear" / Gusto/Starday

1977

Hank Williams / *24 Greatest Hits* /
Polydor/MGM
The Statler Brothers / *The Best of the Statler
Brothers* / Phonogram/Mercury
Waylon Jennings / *Dreaming My Dreams* /
RCA
*Waylon Jennings / *Ol' Waylon* / RCA
Waylon Jennings / *Are You Ready for the
Country* / RCA
Kenny Rogers / *Kenny Rogers* / UA
Glen Campbell / *Southern Nights* / Capitol
Johnny Cash / *The Johnny Cash Portrait/
His Greatest Hits, Vol. III* / Columbia
Glen Campbell / "Southern Nights" / Capitol
Ronnie McDowell / "The King Is Gone" / UA
Kenny Rogers / "Lucille" / UA
Crystal Gayle / "Don't It Make My Brown
Eyes Blue" / UA

1978

Waylon Jennings / *Waylon Live* / RCA
*Waylon Jennings & Willie Nelson / *Waylon
and Willie* / RCA
Ronnie Milsap / *It Was Almost Like a Song* /
RCA

*Freddy Fender's "Before the Next Teardrop
Falls" was certified gold in 1975.*

*Kenny Rogers / *Ten Years of Gold* / UA
Willie Nelson / *The Sound in Your Mind* /
Columbia
Dolly Parton / *The Best of Dolly Parton* /
RCA
Bonnie Tyler / *It's a Heartache* / RCA
*Willie Nelson / *Stardust* / Columbia
Emmylou Harris / *Elite Hotel* / Warner Bros.
*Crystal Gayle / *We Must Believe in Magic* /
UA
*Dolly Parton / *Here You Come Again* / RCA
Dolly Parton / "Here You Come Again" / RCA
Bonnie Tyler / "It's a Heartache" / RCA
Crystal Gayle / *When I Dream* / UA
Anne Murray / "You Needed Me" / Capitol
Waylon Jennings / *I've Always Been
Crazy* / RCA
Ronnie Milsap / *Only One Love in My Life* /
RCA
Anne Murray / *Let's Keep It That Way* /
Capitol
Dolly Parton / *Heartbreaker* / RCA
Kenny Rogers / *Love or Something Like It* /
UA

1979

*Charlie Daniels Band / *Million Mile
Reflection* / Epic
Anne Murray / *New Kind of Feeling* /
Capitol
*Waylon Jennings / *Greatest Hits* / RCA
Ronnie Milsap / *Ronnie Milsap Live* / RCA
Willie Nelson / *Willie Nelson and Family
Live* / Columbia
Willie Nelson/Leon Russell / *One for the
Road* / Columbia
Dolly Parton / *Great Balls of Fire* / RCA
Tanya Tucker / *TNT* / MCA
Charlie Daniels Band / "The Devil Went
Down to Georgia" / Epic
*Kenny Rogers / *The Gambler* / UA
Kenny Rogers / "She Believes in Me" / Epic
Kenny Rogers & Dottie West / *Classics* / UA

*Platinum albums
List courtesy of the Country Music Association

THE BOYS
IN THE BAND

Everybody knows the stars, but hardly anybody knows the bands. Here are the names of some famous country bands. Name the bandleader of each.

1. The Drifting Cowboys
2. The Coal Miners
3. The Buckaroos
4. The Waylors
5. The Do-Rites
6. The Texas Troubadours
7. The Bluegrass Boys
8. The Cherokee Cowboys
9. The Wagonmasters
10. The Musical Brownies
11. The Texas Playboys
12. The Po' Boys
13. The Tennessee Two

14. The Strangers
15. The Golden West Cowboys
16. The Smoky Mountain Boys
17. The Brazos Valley Boys
18. The Light Crust Dough Boys
19. The Hot Band
20. The Foggy Mountain Boys
21. The Cherry Bombs
22. The Band of Thieves
23. The Texas Jewboys
24. The Storytellers
25. The Possum Hunters

ANSWERS

1. Hank Williams
2. Loretta Lynn
3. Buck Owens
4. Waylon Jennings
5. Barbara Mandrell
6. Ernest Tubb
7. Bill Monroe
8. Ray Price
9. Porter Wagoner
10. Milton Brown
11. Bob Wills
12. Bill Anderson
13. Johnny Cash
14. Merle Haggard
15. Pee Wee King
16. Roy Acuff
17. Hank Thompson
18. W. Lee O'Daniel
19. Emmylou Harris
20. Lester Flatt and Earl Scruggs
21. Rodney Crowell
22. Kris Kristofferson
23. Kinky Friedman
24. Tom T. Hall
25. Dr. Humphrey Bate

The original Texas Playboys. Back row: Leon Rausch, vocals; Eldon Shamblin, guitar; Smoky Dacus, drums. Front row: Leon McAuliffe, steel; Keith Coleman, fiddle.

TWENTY GOOD BOOKS

As with records, a country music reading library should function as a source of entertainment as well as knowledge. Therefore, instead of listing every book ever written about the subject, I have selected twenty—including biographies, histories, and, in one case, fiction—that are informative and enjoyable. Some of these books are more difficult to find than others, and for information on hard-to-find books, check your local library or write to the Country Music Foundation, 4 Music Square East, Nashville, Tennessee 37203. Many of these titles are available for sale in the gift shop at the Country Music Hall of Fame and Museum in Nashville, which is located at the same address.

This book, by the way, isn't included on the list; you already know how good it is.

Artis, Bob. *Bluegrass.* New York: Hawthorn, 1975.

This is the best-written and most interesting history of bluegrass yet published. Artis not only tells what happened when, but gives the reader an insight into the personalities of bluegrass musicians such as Bill Monroe, Lester Flatt and Earl Scruggs, Ralph and Carter Stanley, and others. Along the way, you'll find that bluegrass music and bluegrass people are a lot more interesting than you may have imagined.

Delmore, Alton. *Truth Is Stranger Than Publicity.* Edited by Charles Wolfe. Nashville: Country Music Foundation Press, 1977.

This unfinished autobiography by Alton Delmore, half of the popular Delmore Brothers, is probably the earliest attempt (he started it around 1958) any country musician made at writing the story of his or her life. The narrative is strongest when dealing with the thirties, when the Delmores joined, and later left, the Grand Ole Opry; toured with Uncle Dave Macon; and met some strange characters on the road. Funny and sad, the book is more revealing about people than musical history, but that's one of the things that make it fun to read.

Flippo, Chet. *Your Cheatin' Heart.* New York: Simon and Schuster, 1981.

I have to be honest and explain that Chet

Flippo is my husband, but I'd like this biography about Hank Williams even if he weren't. Written in a novelistic style, Flippo doesn't back away from the sordid side of Hank's life (and there was one), and so the reader will learn not only about Hank's triumphs, but also about his booze, pills, fights with his mother and his wives, and his mysterious death. If you're a devoted Hank fan who doesn't want to know about these things, don't read this book. Pretty, it's not.

Fox, William Price. *Ruby Red.* New York: J. B. Lippincott, 1971.

This is the only work of fiction on country music that I consider worth reading. It's the story of one Ruby Jean Jamison of Columbia, South Carolina, and her dream of being on the Grand Ole Opry. On the way, Ruby Jean runs into some very interesting characters, including Jimmie Lee Rideout, a songwriter, and Preacher Roebuck Alexander, who are fictional, and Johnny Cash and Ernest Tubb, who aren't.

Green, Douglas B. *Country Roots: The Origins of Country Music.* New York: Hawthorn, 1976.

While Bill Malone's book (see below) is considered to be more authoritative, Doug Green's is more interesting and entertaining. It's also a bit easier for the nonscholar to understand, since Green breaks the history down by topic (i.e., bluegrass, comedy, western swing) rather than chronologically. There are lots of funny stories and good pictures as well. The one country history to own.

Grissum, John. *Country Music: White Man's Blues.* New York: Paperback Library, 1970.

This book is really a series of sketches, collected in 1969 and 1970 by Grissum, a freelance writer who had written mostly rock stories for *Rolling Stone* magazine prior to this book. Grissum's rock experience, however, brings a fresh perspective to the book, which was one of the first to reveal that country music stars drank, drugged, and copulated, in addition to being on the Grand Ole Opry. There are especially good chapters on Johnny Cash, Waylon Jennings, Merle Haggard, and Buck Owens.

Guralnick, Peter. *Lost Highways: Journeys and Arrivals of American Musicians.* Boston: David Godine, 1979.

Peter Guralnick is one of America's best music writers, and this book of sketches of encounters with musicians like Ernest Tubb, Waylon Jennings, Hank Snow, Deford Bailey, Charlie Rich, Sleepy LaBeef, Mickey Gilley, Merle Haggard, and several other practitioners of straight country, blues, and rockabilly music will show you why. It's also interesting to read after Grissum's and Hemphill's books, because Guralnick's work serves as a sequel to those volumes, showing what became of some of the characters in the former books ten years later.

Haggard, Merle, with Peggy Russell. *Sing Me Back Home: My Life.* New York: Times Books, 1981.

This is the most pessimistic autobiography I've read since *Confessions of a Superfluous Man* by A. J. Nock. *Nothing* good ever happened to poor ole Merle, at least to hear him tell it. Nonetheless, his stories about prison, music, several wives, and an unrequited love affair with Dolly Parton will keep the reader turning the pages. Warning: the book contains a good dose of vulgar language.

Hemphill, Paul. *Bright Lights and Country Music: The Nashville Sound.* New York: Simon and Schuster, 1970.

This book is supposed to serve as a kind of history of country music, but like Grissum's book Hemphill's work represents one of the earlier attempts of non-country-music writers to introduce this strange new thing to the world. Hemphill's sketches cover Tootsie's Orchid Lounge, Bakersfield, recording sessions at Bradleys' Barn, and Glen Campbell, among other stars. All of it is interesting.

Horstman, Dorothy. *Sing Your Heart Out, Country Boy.* New York: E. P. Dutton, 1975.

This annotated collection of classic country song lyrics is being reissued by the Country Music Foundation Press and should be available soon. The songs are divided and cataloged according to topic—home, lost love, traveling, etc.—and each is accompanied by a paragraph from the songwriter explaining how the song came to be written. I have found this to be an invaluable reference work as well as a source of fun.

Lynn, Loretta, with George Vecsey. *Coal Miner's Daughter.* New York: Warner Books, 1976.

This as-told-to autobiography has become a classic of country music literature. Loretta's genuine openness and lack of self-consciousness give the reader a real insight into her personality and into the day-to-day life of a girl singer. You've seen the movie—now read the book.

Malone, Bill. *Country Music, U.S.A.: A Fifty-Year History.* Austin, Texas: University of Texas Press, 1968.

This is universally considered to be the best and most comprehensive country music history yet written. Although I've read this book several times, I've never read it straight through, preferring instead to dip into it at random. The book does have some flaws: its treatment of women is hasty (there's only one sentence on Patsy Cline, for example), and the writing style is too pedantic to be truly popular. The book is also badly in need of revision. Still, it remains the required starting place in the education of a country music scholar.

Porterfield, Nolan. *Jimmie Rodgers.* Urbana, Illinois: University of Illinois Press, 1979.

Since this is the only real biography of Jimmie Rodgers, it's the best by default. Some reviewers, however, consider this to be the best country music biography to have been written, period. Porterfield's exhaustively researched book tells the story of the early country music industry as well as the story of Jimmie Rodgers. An excellent book even for those who aren't terribly interested in country music.

Shelton, Robert, and Burt Goldblatt. *The Country Music Story.* New York: Bobbs Merrill, 1966.

This history of country music is more notable for its pictures than its prose, but its pictures are so interesting and so varied that I'd buy the book for them alone.

Stambler, Irwin, and Landon Grelun. *Encyclopedia of Folk, Country, and Western Music.* New York: St. Martin's, 1969.

This is a handy, if incomplete, reference book, which gives basic biographical sketches of hundreds of musicians. Although there is no analysis of anyone's career, the information included is generally accurate up until the year the book was published. A good book to keep by the stereo for fast reference when needed.

Tosches, Nick. *Country: The Biggest Music in America.* New York: Stein and Day, 1977.

Not to put too fine a point on it, some minor episodes in this entertaining book (such as the one in which the author meets a "famous country star" who's had a sex-change operation) are total fabrications. The stuff that is true, however, is very good reading indeed. This book contains the best piece ever written about Jerry Lee Lewis, as well as some extremely curious and informative revelations about recorded oddities like country songs about sex and country songs that are frankly racist. This is another book which can be taken up and dipped into at will.

Townsend, Charles. *San Antonio Rose: The Life and Music of Bob Wills.* Urbana, Illinois: University of Illinois Press, 1976.

If anyone who's read this book would like to know anything more about Bob Wills, I'd like to know what it is. This is the definitive biography of "the King of Western Swing," and required reading for swing fans.

Williams, Roger M. *Sing a Sad Song: The Life of Hank Williams.* Garden City, New York: Doubleday, 1970.

This book comes as close as any to being the "official" biography of Hank Williams. It's well researched and well written, but short on emotions. I'd suggest you read both this and Flippo's book to get the complete Hank story. But then I *would* suggest that, wouldn't I?

Wolfe, Charles. *Grand Ole Opry: The Early Years, 1925–1935.* London: Old Time Music, 1975.

This is a scholarly, but fascinating, histo-

ry of the founding and early life of the Grand Ole Opry, including pictures, reproductions of newspaper clippings, and posters, and lots of information for trivia collectors.

Wynette, Tammy, with Joan Dew. *Stand By Your Man.* New York: Simon and Schuster, 1978.

The last is certainly not the least, for *Stand By Your Man* is my favorite country music book of all time. In fact, I've read it four times. Tammy leaves nothing out. She tells all about her terrifying first marriage and the other four as well. She tells all about her affairs, including the time poor Burt Reynolds nearly drowned in her bathtub. She tells about George Jones and what it was like to make love to "the Greatest Country Singer in the World" for the first time. She tells about the mysterious fires that drove her from her Nashville mansion. She doesn't tell about the time she was supposedly kidnapped. Aw, Tammy!

OUTTAKES

Time for the tall pines to pine
The paw paws to paw
The bumble bees to bumble all around
The grasshopper hops and the eavesdropper drops
While gently the old cow slips away
This is your reporter, George D. Hay, inviting you to be with us again next
Saturday night.
> —*George D. Hay at the end of each Opry broadcast*

Nobody's perfect. The only one who ever was, was crucified.
> —*Loretta Lynn*

I couldn't go pop with a mouthful of firecrackers.
> —*Waylon Jennings*

Gram (Parsons) always resisted the term "country-rock" because it implied to
him something that was less than the sum of the two. What he was trying to do
was something that was greater than the sum of the two.
> —*Emmylou Harris*

I'm movin' on. I'm headin' for Texas to get my young boys. Why don't you come
along?
> —*Marshall Chapman*

The first song I ever learned to play on the autoharp was "Little Brown Jug."
Most people in them days just strummed it. They didn't realize they was a tune
in it, I don't reckon.
>   —_Mother Maybelle Carter_

I have driven sometimes two nights and two days and never even went to bed.
When we'd get into a town early in the mornin' and they were asleep, I'd put
them to bed and then I'd start workin' on their clothes. I never would let 'em go
on stage wrinkled or anything, so I'd have to wash and iron and everything. By
the time I'd get through, I wouldn't have any time for rest myself, so I'd just go
on and work.
>   —_Mother Maybelle Carter, on traveling with her children,_
>   _the "Second" Carter Family_

I think people have grown away from hillbilly music. The world has changed.
They're not too many of us who can identify anymore with Butcher Holler.
There are far more of us who come from a middle or suburban kind of
background, and we've got our little memories too.
>   —_Lynn Anderson_

I thought it was nothin' but just glamour—you get up there and you sing a few
songs and that's it, and somebody waits on you hand and foot. I didn't dare
think of ridin' two or three hundred miles with rollers in my hair, tryin' to sleep
on the bus and gettin' out at truck stops and eatin' hot dogs and hamburgers.
That didn't enter my mind.
>   —_Tammy Wynette_

It's a picture in the center of Georgette, and I'm over here and George is here.
Underneath mine, he's got, "This house holds lots of old memories. There are
good ones and bad ones, I fear. But nothin' can harm us in this house we
know, 'cause my darlin' Tammy sleeps here." Under Georgette's picture, it has,
"On October the fifth, 1970, my Tamala Georgette has come. When young love
is in bloom and she's happy, I hope you love her as I loved her. Mom."
Underneath his, it says, "When my hair is turned to silver, and affection no
longer flows, it is this I ask of you Tammy: Will you love me when I'm old?"
>   —_Tammy Wynette, describing the plaque George Jones_
>   _made for her when Tamala Georgette was born_

It helps to know how to dance. The music—there's a difference in the timing of
a march time. You would play the number for a march in the Army, and it
would be fast—stepping off. But if you played the Dead March, like I play, it's
different. You're playing the march while they're taking the dead to his grave,
you see, and it goes slow.
>   —_Bill Monroe, on rhythm_

Maybe I was a slave driver, but if a man's going to work for you and you want him to play your music, he has to do what you say. And if it seemed like a slave driver, you'd just have to do that.
—Bill Monroe, on managing a band

I love fox hounds. I love to hear 'em run as they give their mouth, as they bark behind the fox. There's lots of dogs that's got wonderful mouths. They got a high tenor voice or a deep sharp or they'd bark like a turkey, or some had screamin' mouths—put 'em all together, it makes wonderful sound.
—Bill Monroe, on where he gets ideas for his music

Just 'cause I wear a hat ain't got a thing to do with where my head's at.
—Billy Joe Shaver

You're not really a star unless you shine, and I mean shine from all the prongs that's on a star.
—Dolly Parton

I'll make Liberace look like Ned in the first reader.
—Dolly Parton

I am a brave little soldier. I may not win the war, but I'll sure fight like it.
—Dolly Parton

I been hungry too many times and I remember the times. These people have fed me. I won't ever forget it.
—Loretta Lynn, on her fans

I know if I could look in the mirror and I could see myself while I was writin' a story about a woman that is going through torment, I would look like that person. Because I would be living every minute of what that woman lives. And this is what I think makes a songwriter.
—Loretta Lynn

All the interesting women are over thirty.
—Kris Kristofferson

I'd much rather they analyze my songs than my britches.
—Kris Kristofferson, on journalists

I'll pay the piper myself.
—Waylon Jennings

In country music, we want wet eyes, not wet crotches.
—Bobby Bare, explaining the difference between country and rock and roll

APPENDIX

The country music industry has a particularly well-organized system for disseminating information about country's history and its business. Almost any question you may have can be answered by either the Country Music Association or the Country Music Foundation at the addresses listed below. In addition, there are numerous magazines that carry information about current happenings in country music; their addresses are also listed below, as are addresses where would-be songwriters can write for information and where record collectors can get information about rare and out-of-print recordings and memorabilia.

1. The Country Music Business

Billboard, One Astor Plaza, 1515 Broadway, New York, New York 10036. Subscriptions $125.00 per year. Write Billboard Subscription Service Department, P.O. Box 13808, Philadelphia, Pennsylvania 19101.

Billboard is a weekly trade magazine that publishes popularity charts for current records in the pop, black, adult contemporary, gospel, disco, classical, and country fields. There is a news section that accompanies each chart and details current happenings and industry news in each field. The magazine is of use mainly to people who are actually involved in the day-to-day business of music, but others may find it interesting to read the occasional issue. *Billboard* is also available at newsstands in many areas of the country for three dollars per copy.

The Country Music Association, P.O. Box 22299, Nashville, Tennessee 37202 (Phone: 615-244-2840). The Country Music Association—CMA for short—is a country music industry group whose membership is composed of musicians, songwriters, business people, disc jockeys, journalists, and others who make most of their income in a country-music-related field. The CMA acts as a kind of chamber of commerce for the industry, sponsoring the annual CMA Awards, keeping up-to-date information on record companies, bookers, agents, managers, musicians, country radio stations, and the like. The CMA also serves as a public relations agency for the country music business.

The average fan might write to the CMA for record company addresses, lists of country radio stations, information about song publishing, about the Grand Ole Opry, and annual events like Fan Fair and the disc jockey convention.

The Nashville Telephone Book, available by calling the Nashville telephone business office, 615-555-1212.

You can get a copy of Nashville's white and yellow pages simply by calling the above number and requesting one. There will be a charge for the call and perhaps a nominal charge for the book, but it's one of the handiest sources of information around, since it lists the addresses of all record companies, publishing companies, recording studios, and individual stars' offices.

2. Current Happenings in Country Music
The average country music fan can probably find out everything he or she wants to know by subscribing to one or more of the following magazines. All publish news of current happenings in the business, profiles of the stars, gossip columns, record reviews, and book reviews. They are of varying quality, so I suggest you first try them separately, and then pick the one you like best. If you're ever in Nashville, the newsstand at the Country Music Hall of Fame and Museum carries them all.

Country Hotline News, P.O. Box 674, Mt. Juliet, Tennessee 37122. Subscriptions $8.00 per year in the U.S. This magazine, printed on newsprint, runs heavily to gossip.

Country Rhythms, 475 Park Avenue South, New York, New York 10016. Subscriptions $9.98 per year, six issues. This magazine is a newcomer to the field and despite the fact that its editors are equally new to country music, they do a pretty fair job. There are both profiles of current stars and articles about stars of long ago. The articles on current people are rather run-of-the-mill, but

Country Rhythms is lively and has some very nice color pictures.

Country Song Roundup, Charlton Building, Derby, Connecticut 06418. Subscriptions $12.50 per year. *Country Song Roundup* is the granddaddy of all country magazines, and its devoted readership is especially attracted to it because the words to many current hit songs are printed in each issue. There are also profiles, reviews, articles on history, and news of fan clubs. Subscribe without fear.

Country Style, 11058 West Addison St., Franklin Park, Illinois 60131. Subscriptions $12.95 per year. In general, *Country Style* prints gushy, gossipy profiles of the stars, as well as stuff like recipes and psychic predictions. There's the occasional good piece, however, and the occasional off-the-wall story, as well as one article per month of history. The magazine also publishes fan club news.

Music City News, P.O. Box 22975, Nashville, Tennessee 37202. Subscriptions $10.00 per year. *Music City News*, a monthly owned by singer Faron Young, has been in business several years, and is trusted by many fans. As its title implies, it's heavy on Nashville news—especially gossip—and short on star profiles. It's a very good magazine for the hardcore fan, and its fan club coverage is the best.

3. Country Music History
The Country Music Foundation Library and Media Center, 4 Music Square East, Nashville, Tennessee 37203 (Phone: 615-256-1639).

Country fans are very fortunate to have the CMF, as it's called for short. Housed on the lower level of the Country Music Hall of Fame, the CMF has a library that includes printed material, recordings, videotapes, old movies, magazines, photographs, and you name it. If it has to do with country music history, it's probably there.

If you have questions about country music

history, write the CMF and the library staff will try to answer them, though if it's a very complicated question, you may be charged a $10-per-hour research fee. Photocopies of material in the library can also be ordered for ten cents per Xerox copy, or fifteen cents per microfilm copy. A minimum charge of one dollar applies to all orders. Payment on all orders is required in advance of shipping.

It's also possible to visit the CMF if you're in Nashville. You must first know what you want (for example, you might want to see the library's file on Hank Williams, or you might want to hear an old record); and you must call for an appointment at the number listed above. The CMF Library is *not* for browsers or the merely curious. It's for people who want to find specific information.

The Library and Media Center will make copies of recordings and videotapes for those who have a specific use for them—usually professional scholars, writers, and filmmakers only. You can see if you qualify by calling and asking. Don't be afraid—they're very nice people.

The John Edwards Memorial Foundation Folklore and Mythology Center, University of California at Los Angeles, Los Angeles, California 90024 (Phone: 213-825-3777). The JEMF is a foundation administered by UCLA and the executors of the estate of John Edwards, an Australian who was a devoted country music fan and collector. He willed his collection to UCLA and it has been added to over the years. In addition to its function as a research library, the foundation also issues records and pamphlets on country music history, and you can get lists of these pamphlets and records by writing to the above address. One can also visit the JEMF by appointment. Their rules are a bit less stringent than the CMF's, and you're allowed to browse among the shelves. The JEMF's facilities are also smaller than the CMF's, so don't too many of you go at once.

4. Record Collecting

Unfortunately, record companies don't always keep all the records they issue in print forever, and that means that the consumer who wants a specific record often has to hunt for it. Sometimes these people become record collectors and swap and buy and sell rare records as a hobby. In general, however, you can find a lot of out-of-print records at garage sales, fleamarkets, and discount stores like K-Mart. These places have reasonable prices and you'll often find great buys. My husband and I found a mint copy of *Freddy Fender Live at Louisiana State Prison* (made when Freddy was an inmate, not a visitor) at a street sale just recently for only four dollars. Start your search at places like these, then, if you want to get into serious collecting—and to pay serious collectors' prices—try some of these places:

Don Cleary, P.O. Box 16265, Fort Lauderdale, Florida 33318. Cleary runs record auctions by mail, and a copy of his current list is available from the above address. If you become a customer, you'll keep getting the list; if not, he'll cut you off. His selection is huge, but you won't always find the exact item you're looking for. On the other hand, you might find a record you didn't know you wanted before.

County Sales, Box 191, Floyd, Virginia 24091. This mail-order record outlet and record label, administered by Dave Freeman, specializes in old-time music. *County* stocks copies of records on its own label as well as hard-to-find recordings on labels like Old Timey, Arhoolie, Yazoo, Charly, JEMF, Voyager, and so forth. They are the last word for stringband, bluegrass, and fiddle music.

Goldmine Magazine, Box 187, Fraser, Michigan 48026. Subscriptions $20 per year. *Goldmine* is a magazine just for record collectors. The magazine doesn't specialize in country music, but its advertising section carries column after column of people who do, and who want to swap, sell, or buy country records.

Doug Hanners, 1316 Kenwood, Austin, Texas 78757. Also in business for himself, Hanners will search for specific records for you if you write him at the above address. If he can find them, he'll sell them to you. If he can't there's no charge. Usually, Doug can find anything. His prices are very reasonable, but very rare records can be prohibitively expensive, so make sure you really want a record before writing.

5. *Information for Songwriters*

Sometimes it seems that there are more amateur songwriters out there than you can shake a stick at, and every one of them is just positive that if (name any singer) could just hear his or her song, it would be a smash hit. Friends, this only happens in the movies. Still, since songwriters often get ripped off, they should educate themselves about how to copyright songs and about what publishing contracts look like.

Begin by buying a copy of *This Business Of Music* by Sidney Shemel and M. William Krasilovsky (New York: Billboard Publications, 1980). It's available at most bookstores, but be sure you get the latest edition with the 1980 copyright law included. This book is complicated but it's invaluable.

You can also order a pamphlet called "What Every Songwriter Should Know" by writing the Country Music Association at the address listed at the beginning of this section.

Finally, *don't send tapes to me.* I wouldn't say this except for the fact that some people have, in the mistaken idea that I have some pull. I don't. No pull whatsoever. I will probably lose your tape.

(*Note:* The subscription prices listed for magazines in this section may have changed by the time you read this. Check to make sure before ordering.)